Information Systems Engineering Library

GEMINI: Managing KBS Development Projects

Guidance for IS-provider project managers

Frances Scarff

Judith Fynn

CCTA

November 1993

LONDON: HMSO

First published 1993

ISBN 0 11 330592 3

For further information regarding this publication and other CCTA products please contact:

CCTA Library
Riverwalk House
157-161 Millbank
London SW1P 4RT

071-217-3331

Contents

Foreword

The **Information Systems Engineering Library** provides guidance on managing and carrying out Information Systems Engineering activities. In the IS life cycle, Information Systems Engineering takes place once the IS strategy has been defined. It is concerned with the development and ongoing improvement of information systems up to the operational stage, when systems become the responsibility of infrastructure management.

The Information Systems Engineering Library builds on guidance in the CCTA IS Guides, particularly set A: *Management and Planning Set* and set B: *Systems Development Set* and complements other CCTA products, in particular the project management method, PRINCE, and the systems analysis and design method, SSADM.

Volumes in the Information Systems Engineering Library are of interest to varying levels of staff from IS directors to IS providers, helping them to improve the quality and productivity of their IS development work. Some volumes in this library should also be of interest to business managers, IS users and those involved in market testing, whose business operations depend on having effective IS support by means of Information Systems Engineering activities.

The Information Systems Engineering Library also complements other related CCTA publications, particularly the IT Infrastructure Library for operational issues and the IS Planning Subject Guides for strategic issues.

CCTA welcomes customer views on Information Systems Engineering Library publications. Please send your comments to:

Customer Services
Information Systems Engineering Group
Gildengate House
Upper Green Lane
NORWICH
NR3 1DW

Acknowledgements

The GEMINI guidance has been developed using a wide range of expertise from the following:

Chris Harris-Jones and David Hannaford from BIS Information Systems Ltd.

Mark Thomas and Ebbi Adhami from Ernst & Young Management Consultants.

Paul Shufflebottom from LBMS plc.

Jim Kennedy from Logica (Cambridge Ltd).

Richard Susskind from Masons.

Gary Borne from SD-Scicon.

Frank Hickman, Jonathan Killin and Lise Land from Touche Ross Management Consultants.

Contributions have been made by reviewers from a wide range of Government Departments including:

Department of Health

Department of Trade and Industry

HM Customs and Excise

Inland Revenue

ITSA

MOD AQUILA

Contributions have been made by reviewers from academic institutions including:

AIAI

Liverpool University (Dept. of Computer Science)

Contributions have been made by reviewers from a wide range of commercial organisations including:

British Aerospace

British Telecom (Martlesham Heath)

Inference (Europe)

Norwich Union

Siemens Nixdorf Information Systems

1 Introduction

1.1 Purpose

This publication is intended to give IS providers responsible for managing KBS development activities an understanding of the key issues involved and the steps they should take to ensure these are addressed.

Development projects for *knowledge based systems* (KBS) require the use of novel analysis and design techniques.

Often, the business requirement cannot be easily described and rigorously defined at the start of a project. The development process frequently involves an iterative approach to knowledge acquisition, requirements analysis and design. KBS projects are therefore not fully amenable to conventional methods for development and project management. IS providers have an obligation to use their professionalism to help the business customer to realise the business requirements.

The purpose of the GEMINI volumes of the Information Systems Engineering Library is to help organisations adapt their project practices for KBS development. Within GEMINI, the analysis and design elements are based on good practice for KBS development. The project management approach is based on the government preferred project management method PRojects IN Controlled Environments (PRINCE).

Organisations which use a project management method other than PRINCE will need to identify how their approach needs to be modified to allow it to be used in conjunction with this guidance.

1.2 Who should read this publication

This publication is primarily intended for use by *project managers who are responsible, as IS providers, for supplying KBS development products to a user organisation.* The guidance is also relevant to *project managers who are supplying KBS development expertise.*

They need to know the relevant issues in KBS projects and be able to check that such projects are carried out within the given constraints, and satisfy business requirements.

The publication is also likely to be of interest to:

- individuals in government organisations who have some responsibility for KBS development projects
- Project Assurance Team members
- KBS Development Team members.

All of these groups need to communicate with the Project Manager. This publication will help them to understand the role and responsibilities of a Project Manager within a KBS development project and should facilitate effective communication.

1.3 Structure of the publication

The focus is on the issues which a Project Manager needs to address within a KBS development project.

Chapter 2 provides an overview of GEMINI concepts and structure.

Chapter 3 describes the project organisation for a KBS development project from the IS-provider perspective.

Chapters 4 to 9 provide guidance on the subjects of project management, project quality management, risk management, planning, production management and project integration.

The annexes provide additional detail.

1.4 How to use this publication

The GEMINI guidance provides a framework for undertaking KBS development projects. It is designed to be flexible rather than prescriptive and is intended to be adapted to the particular needs of the organisations which use it and of the projects to which it is applied.

This publication offers guidance to Project Managers within an IS provider organisation. It helps them understand the aspects of KBS development projects which need to be given particular attention. Project management should be carried out by a Project Manager with project management experience and a KBS background.

GEMINI includes PRINCE concepts, tailored for KBS development projects, and some additional concepts. It is assumed that the reader has knowledge of PRINCE. A full explanation of the method is available in the PRINCE manuals.

Organisations which use a project management method other than PRINCE will need to determine how their approach needs to be modified to allow it to be used in conjunction with this guidance.

Initially, readers are recommended to read the whole publication. Subsequently, it can be referenced as a reminder of issues that need to be addressed.

GEMINI should be scaled appropriately for each project.

1.5 GEMINI publications

This publication is one of three volumes which together form the foundation volumes of GEMINI guidance, within the CCTA Information System Engineering (ISE) Library. The others are:

- *GEMINI: Controlling KBS Development Projects - Guidance for business-side project controllers*
- *GEMINI Technical Reference - Guidance for KBS development project teams.*

Each of these volumes is intended to be self contained; therefore, some information is duplicated across the volumes. Each volume holds an appropriate level of detail for its purpose.

Each volume contains an index which can help to:

- direct the reader to specific text
- identify duplicated coverage of information on a particular topic.

Although GEMINI has been produced as guidance for KBS development, many of the concepts can be applied to other projects which are innovative, risk prone and require iterative development. However, when GEMINI is used for non-KBS projects, it must be tailored to fit those projects. The KBS-specific products, development activities and techniques defined in GEMINI will need to be redefined appropriately for the type of project.

The GEMINI publications contain general concepts which are explained more fully in other publications. Information on these concepts is included in the GEMINI publications to set the context and reduce the need for reference to other documents, especially the PRINCE manuals. Some of the relevant CCTA publications are described in section 1.6.

GEMINI: Controlling KBS Development Projects

GEMINI: Controlling KBS Development Projects defines the roles that are required for KBS projects, in addition to the standard PRINCE roles. It gives an understanding of the key issues involved in controlling the development of KBS and the steps needed to ensure these are addressed. *GEMINI: Controlling KBS Development Projects* is addressed primarily at the business user organisation.

GEMINI Technical Reference

GEMINI Technical Reference provides technical information to enable KBS developers to contribute to or work within a project being run according to the GEMINI guidance. The products and development activities need to be tailored for individual KBS projects.

The *GEMINI Technical Reference* publication sets out what KBS development practitioners are expected to produce during a project which is undertaken according to GEMINI guidance.

1.6 Other publications of interest

Other CCTA publications may be of interest to those using GEMINI guidance. These include the Appraisal and Evaluation Library which includes a volume specific to KBS software tools. Other related publications are concerned with the PRINCE project management method, quality management, CCTA Risk Analysis and Management Method (CRAMM) and the IT Infrastructure Library (ITIL).

PRINCE Manuals

PRINCE is the recommended project management method for use in government. It comprises an integrated set of procedures based on a number of key principles. There is a set of five manuals which document the PRINCE approach to project management.

Some PRINCE concepts have been detailed in GEMINI to limit the requirement to reference the PRINCE manuals. For those not familiar with PRINCE, further information may be needed to allow a complete understanding of the project management principles embodied in GEMINI.

CCTA Appraisal and Evaluation Library

The CCTA Appraisal and Evaluation Library helps organisations to identify the products, particularly software, which best meet their requirements. It consists of a general procedures volume, which describes an appraisal and evaluation 'method', followed by a number of technology specific volumes. There is a volume on KBS, which provides a hierarchy of criteria that may be used as the basis for the evaluation of KBS tools.

CRAMM	CRAMM provides a structured and consistent basis to identify and justify all the protective measures necessary to ensure the security of both current and future IT systems used for processing data. CRAMM can be used within a KBS development project to establish requirements and constraints associated with security.
CCTA IT Infrastructure Library	The IT Infrastructure Library (ITIL) is a set of guidance books which give a comprehensive structured approach to providing IT services and the accommodation and environmental facilities needed to support IT. The publications bring together best IT practices within the public and private sector. These documents cover a variety of subjects, some of which are of direct relevance to GEMINI, including: • Capacity Management • Change Management • Configuration Management • Testing an IT Service for Operational Use.
Quality Management Library	The Quality Management Library provides guidance on implementing and supporting quality management systems (QMS) within IS organisations.

2 Overview

2.1 Introduction

Projects to develop KBS need a particularly rigorous management approach and have highlighted the limitations of conventional IS-development methods.

GEMINI provides a framework for the development of KBS which embodies good practice to reduce the risks of using novel analysis and design techniques and an iterative development approach.

This chapter sets out the key issues involved in developing knowledge-based systems and describes a framework for managing the development activities. The issues addressed are of major significance to Project Managers who are required to:

- manage IS-provider development staff
- co-ordinate activities with the demand side, in particular delivery of the technical products.

2.2 Considerations for KBS development

There are three fundamental characteristics of KBS development projects that prevent conventional methods from fully meeting the needs of these projects:

- special techniques are required for knowledge acquisition and representation
- the activities of feasibility study, requirements definition, analysis and design may overlap
- KBS development projects are generally innovative and thus, particularly susceptible to risk.

In any information systems development, there is a progression from defining what the IS customer - the *demand side* - needs, to how the systems are actually provided by the *supply side.*

Within a KBS project the supply side activities may be provided by one organisation, several different ones in parallel or different ones sequentially. The supply side must work within the overall control of the demand side to ensure that the project is properly managed and co-ordinated so that customers get what they need.

2.2.1 Special techniques

The analysis of knowledge and translation of the results of the analysis into the design of a system, involves the use of specialised techniques, especially in the area of elicitation and representation of knowledge. These techniques are not yet widely known, understood and standardised.

As the supply side and the demand side are likely to be operating in quite separate specialist disciplines, their cultures and language may be very different.

The situation just described often results in a pronounced schism between supply and demand sides. This schism increases the complexity of project management and highlights the importance of a clearly defined, mutually understood, interface between the demand side and the supply side.

The supply side may be required to advise the demand side on the availability of various techniques and their suitability for each of the development activities. Alternatively, the demand side may leave the choice of techniques to the supply side. In either case the demand side will need to understand any implications of the choice of techniques for demand side involvement in development.

2.2.2 Overlapping activities

KBS developers often find it impossible to separate the processes of analysis, design and implementation into a clean linear sequence, as required by a waterfall lifecycle. Some revision of the design and the analysis products may occur late in the project as the scope and limitations of the knowledge emerge. Even the requirements, feasibility and scope of the system may have to be revised at a relatively late stage in the project.

Each product of the development project depends on the availability of information required as input to the appropriate development activity, often from another product. This type of dependency between products needs to be identified. The ordering and conduct of activities should be determined by the characteristics, dependencies and needs of individual projects.

The supply side must provide information to satisfy the demand side that progress and resource usage are within plans and tolerances, so that the demand side can monitor the project and retain overall control.

2.2.3 Project risk

The successful use of KBS can result in great benefits in business areas previously intractable to IT. Many conventional systems meet the needs of the support functions of business.

An unacceptably high proportion of KBS projects fail to deliver operational systems, which meet business requirements, to time and within budget.

KBS developments require the use of innovative technologies. These technologies are inherently risk prone but can deliver valuable benefits when used successfully.

KBS developments are often intended to meet the needs of executive functions fundamental to achieving business aims. If the KBS were to give imperfect information or fail to perform the desired function adequately, this could prove detrimental to the whole business.

Many conventional project management methods incorporate elements of risk management, though these elements are often not openly described. KBS developments require risk analysis and re-planning to be made explicit in the project management process.

2.3 GEMINI guidance

GEMINI guidance focuses on the organisational and planning framework to control KBS developments, with the aim of addressing the areas where conventional methods fail to tackle the issues highlighted in section 2.2.

GEMINI provides a flexible approach for management and control which incorporates continuous risk management and allows the development team to employ the techniques and methods appropriate to the project. The scope of GEMINI encompasses Feasibility Study through to design, covering the issues specific to KBS. The guidance must be tailored to fit existing standards for the demand side organisation and to meet the needs of individual projects.

Key design features of GEMINI include:

- usability
- flexibility
- rigour
- quality.

2.3.1 Usability

The test of any guidance is the extent to which it is found useful in practice. Therefore, the design aim is to ensure that the GEMINI guidance:

- is *understandable* for those with a background in conventional IT
- can be widely *taught* and easily *learned*
- is *applicable* in a wide range of different situations: for example, it is able to address different business problems, or different technical constraints
- is *tailorable* so that the activities carried out are relevant to the project in question.

2.3.2 Flexibility

GEMINI provides a flexible approach for management and control which incorporates continuous risk management. It also allows the development staff to employ the techniques and methods most appropriate to the project.

2.3.3 Rigour

GEMINI is designed to allow:

- project objectives to be set, linking demonstrably to business objectives
- products, which support project objectives, to be identified during planning
- product development to be monitored and documented, which helps to ensure that products are developed efficiently and economically
- risks to project objectives to be rigorously assessed and effectively controlled.

2.3.4 Quality

GEMINI embodies good practice in KBS development. Management techniques used for conventional developments are adopted, where appropriate, and if necessary enhanced.

GEMINI emphasises the management of quality. Quality is achieved by identifying:

- what needs to be produced
- how production will be undertaken
- activities to be scheduled, with particular reference to quality review.

Everyone involved in the project should be aware of these requirements and their part in the quality assurance process.

2.4 Using GEMINI

Using GEMINI involves substantial preparatory work, mostly by the demand side, in the early stages of a project. This work sets the baseline and the framework for the project which will then be driven by:

- an understanding and assessment of objectives and constraints
- the assessment and management of risk
- the assessment and management of quality.

The demand side objective is to gain the most appropriate system to meet the business need, within business constraints. Achieving this objective requires that the demand side exercise tight control over the project and get heavily involved in its development.

The supply side must meet the demand side requirements and provide support to the demand side management by exercising control over the development staff activities and providing information for the demand side project management activities.

2.5 The GEMINI components

The following key elements are incorporated in GEMINI:

- a project organisation structure
- a project management process model with risk management fully integrated
- a product-oriented framework to identify the products to be developed and the activities to develop them.

2.5.1 Project organisation structure

A GEMINI-based project has a clearly defined management environment. The project organisation identifies the skills and experience required to undertake all the necessary project functions concerning control, management and development.

Information flows across a clearly defined, mutually understood, interface, and enables user needs to be met satisfactorily and quickly at each stage.

A project organisation structure is detailed in Chapter 3.

2.5.2 Project management process model

Project management is concerned with the deployment and control of all resources assigned to the project to ensure efficient and economic delivery of effective systems.

Rigorous risk management has been incorporated into GEMINI because KBS developments are more threatened by risks than many conventional IT projects. Project staff using the guidance are required to carry out risk assessment in a regular controlled way, then consider and manage the identified risks. After each risk assessment, development work is planned, carried out and reviewed.

Risk management has been incorporated into a process model that takes account of the iterative nature of KBS development. This model of development and the process model are described in Chapter 4.

2.5.3 Product-oriented framework

The framework provided by GEMINI defines the products needed to support the development of KBS. This framework includes products for use in:

- management and control of the project (Management Products)
- translating the initial business requirements through analysis and design into an implemented system (Technical Products)
- quality control (Quality Products).

There are several Technical Products used to document the analysis and design process. Development of one product may depend on the availability of another. By analysing these dependencies a set of activities can be identified and drawn together into a work structure.

The volume *GEMINI Technical Reference* gives additional information on activities and work structures.

GEMINI focuses on the right planning framework to control product development.

The major analysis and design products are described in Chapter 8.

3 Project organisation

3.1 Introduction

A GEMINI-based project needs to be undertaken in a clearly defined project management environment under the control of the demand side. Project success is determined by project organisation and the commitment and calibre of those involved in the project. This chapter explains the issues associated with project organisation for KBS development projects.

The focus, in this chapter, is on the project organisation from the supply side perspective.

3.1.1 Project organisation

Within GEMINI, *project organisation* is the composition of a team in terms of the skills and experience required of each of its members to undertake all the necessary functions of control, management and development within a project. The project functions are assigned to a number of designated roles. These roles are assigned to individuals according to the needs of the project and the mix of skills available. To undertake a role, an individual requires specific skills and experience directly related to the tasks which they are required to perform.

Each individual undertaking a role must:

- have appropriate skills and knowledge for the allocated role
- understand their responsibilities and those of the other project members, which includes understanding the requirements for interaction with other roles
- understand the project organisation structure and reporting lines.

3.1.2 When to address project organisation

The demand side is responsible for ensuring that the correct project organisation is defined and populated, so that it will be able to resolve any problems encountered during system development. Part of this responsibility is to ensure that the individuals put forward from the supply side have appropriate skills and experience to carry out the required development activities. The supply side must put forward suitable individuals and provide relevant information on them, as soon as they are involved in the project.

3.2 Implications for project organisation

Projects undertaken using GEMINI require slightly different project organisation from many conventional IS projects, to address particular characteristics of KBS development:

- lack of established skills and techniques
- communication problems
- the need for close liaison between demand and supply organisations.

Lack of skills

KBS development projects require the project organisation to encompass specialised skills and knowledge.

The business users and experts are unlikely to have any substantial KBS experience. They may have had little contact with any IT development. The supply side need to take this into account when nominating personnel for the project and when estimating the resource requirements.

Communication problems

Close liaison is required between all members of the project team. The individual team members will have differing backgrounds and specialised skills, which can make this liaison difficult. The technical personnel of the supply side must have close involvement with demand side staff during analysis and design. It is a supply side responsibility to ensure that their personnel handle the communications sensitively.

Demand/supply interface

The demand side frequently find difficulty in defining KBS requirements with sufficient precision to allow a realistic estimate of the resources required to meet them. However, a project cannot be initiated with an open commitment to resource use.

The demand side needs to retain control over the total resources used on the project; therefore, it needs a role for the purpose of exercising this control. The person appointed to this role by the demand side is the *Project Controller,* who is responsible for the use of resources within the demand side project.

The supply side provide a *Project Manager,* who is responsible for managing the completion of the supply side involvement to the demand side's satisfaction. This person is responsible for day-to-day management of the development staff. Although the Project Manager is appointed by the supply side, the demand side will need to be convinced of the person's suitability for the role.

These two roles, the Project Controller and the Project Manager, support close liaison across the demand/supply interface.

3.3 Structure of project organisation

This section describes the recommended project organisation for KBS development projects. Details of project roles and responsibilities within that organisation structure are given.

Figure 3.1 illustrates the GEMINI recommended organisation structure and shows the split of functions between the demand side and supply side.

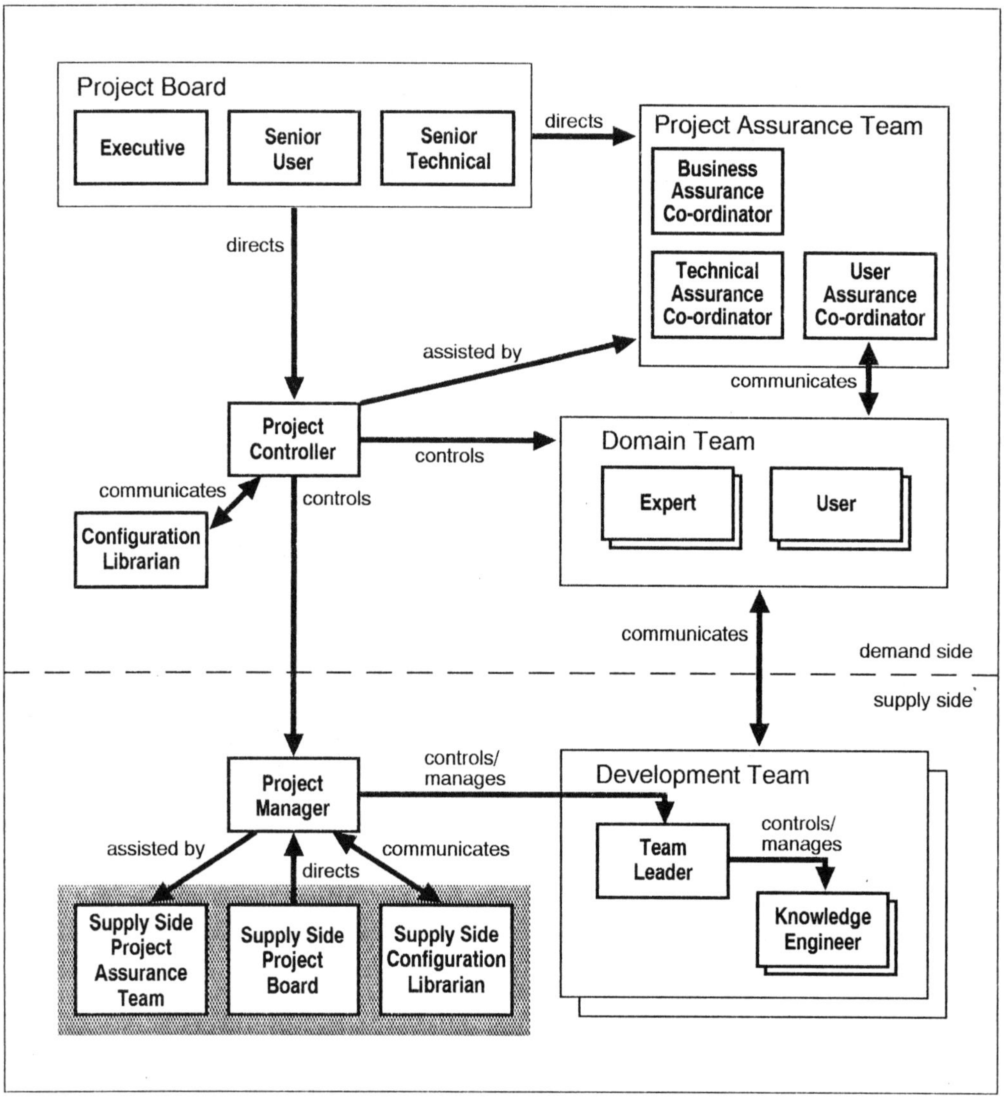

Figure 3.1: Organisation structure for a GEMINI project

A potential need has been established by the demand side. The supply side meet this need, by undertaking development of the full KBS, or some aspect of the development.

The supply side management and development staff are part of the overall project organisation controlled by the demand side. The supply side may also run the work as part of a separate project, within their own organisation. The objectives of this supply side project may be different from those for the overall project but must encompass meeting demand side objectives. A supply side configuration librarian would have responsibility for products under supply side control prior to delivery to the demand side.

This volume concentrates on the overall project. Any discussion of the project organisation in the rest of this volume refers to that controlled by the demand side (it excludes the shaded area of the diagram).

Some of the roles within this section are identical to those defined in PRINCE, and are identified as such. More detail is provided where roles are different from PRINCE ones.

3.3.1 Project Controller

The *Project Controller* acts on behalf of the Project Board, has close links with the board members and attends board meetings. The Project Controller is the demand side project manager responsible for the success of the project in terms of quality of delivered system, budget and timescale. To fulfil these responsibilities, a Project Controller needs to have awareness of the issues particular to KBS developments. Communications skills are also important as this role is central to the project organisation.

The Project Controller aims to ensure the success of the project by controlling the demand/supply interface. This is helped by agreeing how the demand/supply relationship is to operate. The agreement must cover:

- the project organisation structure
- project plans and monitoring
- control mechanisms
- the requirements for delivery of the project products which the supply side will develop.

This information should be documented and should become part of any formal agreement or contract.

The supply side has to work to any agreement or contract and should ensure that the provisions are acceptable to the individuals who have to carry them out.

The Project Controller provides information to the Project Board and controls the supply side Project Manager.

The role of Project Controller is an additional role to those defined by PRINCE. Further information concerning this role can be found in the ISE Library volume *GEMINI: Controlling KBS Development Projects*.

3.3.2 Project Manager

The Project Manager has responsibility for the overall management of the supply side activities with additional responsibility for providing information to the demand side.

This role is similar to the standard PRINCE Project Manager role, except that the liaison with the Project Board is conducted through the Project Controller.

Activities associated with this role include:

- planning the project development activities
- managing resources (including managing risk associated with the development activities)
- monitoring progress and resource usage
- undertaking quality assurance of the products being developed
- liaising with and managing the Development Team, and liaising with the Project Controller and other interested parties as appropriate.

Liaison with the Project Controller may also include taking part in negotiations leading to, and setting up, the agreement which may form part of a formal contract.

Further information is contained in Annexes A and B.

3.3.3 Development Team

A Project Manager is supported by at least one Development Team which is responsible for delivering the products of the project. The team organisation, task definitions and allocation of individuals will depend on the size and nature of the project and the skills required.

The Project Manager is responsible for identifying prospective Development Team members and ensuring that their skills and experience are correctly documented. Before they are assigned the Project Controller must be satisfied that they are suitable for the project. The Project Manager must make provision for replacements to be assigned, in a reasonable timescale, should this become necessary.

These roles have the same overall function as a Development Team on a non-KBS project. The skills required to undertake these functions relate directly to the techniques and technology being employed.

Team Leader

The Team Leader has to manage the development of particular products using specified resources. The functions of the Team Leader are:

- team leadership: the Team Leader will require the skills to lead and co-ordinate a team of Knowledge Engineers. The Team Leader will typically be a working member of the team
- control of delegated budget and resources
- reporting to the Project Manager: the Team Leader must report regularly and therefore needs the skills to assess what must be reported and when
- production of KBS products: the major responsibility of the team leader is to organise the resources within the Development Team so as to produce a designated product, to the required quality, on time and within budget.

The Team Leader must have leadership skills and experience of KBS developments. A thorough knowledge of the relevant aspects of GEMINI, and the techniques and skills for developing the particular products, is essential.

Knowledge Engineer

Knowledge Engineers are the main body of development personnel in a KBS project. There are three principal sub-roles for a Knowledge Engineer. Each of these sub-roles may be carried out by one or more individuals, as follows:

- the *systems analyst* carries out all those activities necessary to produce complete analysis products. Skills required are those for knowledge acquisition, knowledge elicitation, knowledge representation and KBS requirements analysis
- the *designer* takes the analysis products and translates them into a design (both logical and physical)

- the *programmer* works from a physical design and programs the required functionality into the KBS.

3.3.4 Domain Team

The Domain Team is the group of people from the business who have or use the knowledge which the KBS is to contain. The Domain Team provide information for the analysis and design activities carried out by the Development Team. Some of the Domain Team will gain benefit from the project in their day-to day activities once the application has been analysed and built.

The Domain Team roles form an extension to PRINCE. These roles are described briefly, as the skills and requirements to fulfil the roles will vary greatly across projects. The individuals assigned to Domain Team roles will be committed to the overall success of the project. The Project Manager may be required to provide guidance on making choices from candidates for these roles.

There are two groups of Domain Team candidates of particular interest:

- Users
- Experts.

User

The User is the group of users, or their representative, who makes direct use of the final implemented system.

The User has a vital role in the project which may involve:

- being available for requirements analysis
- testing prototypes of the system
- undertaking final system acceptance.

Expert

The Expert is a group of experts, or their representative, who currently performs the function which the system will eventually provide. The Expert must be available to be interviewed for knowledge acquisition and analysis purposes.

The Expert provides the materials, including specialist knowledge, documentation and case studies, that are required by the Knowledge Engineers. In some cases the Expert may be involved in system testing.

Experts may also be prospective users of the final implemented system. The user needs of experts are likely to differ from the needs of other users.

3.3.5 Project Board

The Project Board is a group of senior managers on the demand side who have an interest in, and overall control of, the KBS project.

The function and composition of the Project Board is that advocated within PRINCE.

The members of the Project Board have sufficient authority to commit resources from their appropriate areas, bearing in mind the size and nature of the project. The Project Board members are appointed for the duration of the KBS project.

3.3.6 Project Assurance Team

The Project Assurance Team (PAT) is responsible for ensuring that the products delivered to the demand side are fit for their intended purpose and conform to specification. The PAT must ensure that quality management is undertaken within the project.

The PAT roles are standard PRINCE ones.

3.3.7 Configuration Librarian

The Configuration Librarian is responsible for planning, monitoring and reporting on all configuration management aspects of the project. The identification and version control of products are key functions of configuration management.

This role is defined within the PRINCE manuals.

3.4 Assigning roles

The Project Controller is responsible for ensuring that all roles on the demand side are assigned. The Project Manager is responsible for assigning individuals to the Development Team and must ensure that the individuals concerned have adequate skills for the roles allocated to them. The Project Controller will require evidence of their suitability.

3.5 Summary

The appropriateness of a project organisation structure plays a major part in ensuring the success of a project. The Project Manager is the pivotal supply side role.

At the beginning of supply side involvement in a project, the Project Manager must ensure that:

- effective communication channels have been created within the project
- every role within the supply side, described above, has been assigned to a competent individual who has the relevant skills and knowledge (or ensure that relevant training has been organised)
- the Development Team members are aware of their own and others' roles and responsibilities.

The individual members of the project organisation are important in that failure to fulfil the functions of any single role is likely to jeopardise the chances of success for the whole project.

4 Project management

4.1 Introduction

The objective of this chapter is to define project management in the context of GEMINI, and give guidance to help the Project Manager improve the quality, timeliness and cost effectiveness of KBS development activities. This will be of benefit to both the supply and demand sides of KBS development projects.

The Project Manager bears the principal responsibility for ensuring that effective project management is applied within the supply side for the project. This chapter explains project management issues in such a way as to help the Project Manager carry out this function.

This chapter assumes a knowledge of PRINCE and uses PRINCE terminology. A full explanation of the method is available in the PRINCE manuals.

4.1.1 Project management concepts

Project management is the administration of all resources to develop products which are required to fulfil the objectives of the project.

Products

A *product,* in this context, is any output from a project. It may be an item of software, hardware or documentation and may itself consist of a number of component products. Products are described within three categories:

- *Management Products* which are produced as part of the management of a project
- *Technical Products* which are the results of the project development activities
- *Quality Products* which are produced for or by the quality process.

Chapter 4 of *GEMINI Technical Reference* describes how these products fit together in an exemplar Product Breakdown Structure.

Deliverables	*Deliverables* are those products which must be developed by the supply side and formally accepted by the demand side. Deliverables are defined in terms of content, structure and format so that everyone involved in their development knows what is expected and has confidence that they will be accepted.
Activity	An *activity* is the process of creation or further development of a product. Each time a product is to be created or enhanced, an activity is defined to effect the transformation. Each activity will be conducted using appropriate techniques for that activity. It may be necessary to have work undertaken on several products at the same time. Application of configuration management assists in the control of this process. See Chapter 5 for more details on configuration management.
Project management tasks	Project management is concerned with meeting the project objectives and the business requirements by: • organising resources to ensure that the appropriate equipment and skills are available at the right time • planning the use of these resources to complete the activities which will produce the products • assessing progress and resource utilisation • controlling the technical activities to ensure that products are produced to the appropriate level of quality, on time and to budget • reporting progress on both a routine and ad-hoc basis • taking corrective action when problems are detected • obtaining decisions and approvals from the appropriate level of authority.

4.1.2 Who undertakes project management

The Project Board delegates responsibility for deployment of project resources to managers with technical experience. For the demand side this authority is delegated to the Project Controller who delegates some responsibility to the Project Manager, who delegates some responsibilities further. There are several levels at which project management activities must be undertaken. Each level deploys its own delegated authority. Within the project organisation, detailed in Chapter 3, the levels are:

- Project Board
- Project Controller
- Project Manager
- Team Leader(s).

GEMINI takes the split between demand side and supply side to be at the point of communication between the Project Controller and Project Manager.

It is possible that different approaches to project management will be employed by the demand side and the supply side. There are three scenarios likely to be of interest:

- both organisations follow the GEMINI guidance. Each will understand the interface requirements of the other organisation
- the demand side follows the GEMINI guidance and the supply side does not. In this case, the Project Manager needs to understand the principal concepts within GEMINI to be able to interface appropriately
- the supply side follows the GEMINI guidance and the demand side does not. In this case, the demand side may require information and products to be provided in a specific way, different from GEMINI. The GEMINI principles will be followed during development, but the products will need to be tailored according to the demand side approach.

This guidance recommends that both sides follow GEMINI in order to complete successful projects.

4.2 Considerations for project management

There are a number of features of a KBS development project which demand particular attention from a project management viewpoint.

The large amounts of information and knowledge involved in KBS developments determines how much effort will be involved in analysing the requirement. Initially it is difficult to assess the scale of the analysis task required and the complexity of the knowledge to be analysed. The demand side needs to keep tight control of the progress and resource usage of such a project and be aware of any issues, raised during the analysis of the expertise, which requires any re-focusing of the project.

The techniques of prototyping are frequently used on KBS development projects. This mode of working can quickly consume resources and lose focus. Managing these activities is a priority.

There is a need for a project management approach which is flexible and permits iteration, while maintaining rigour and focus throughout the project.

4.3 Project phases and approach

GEMINI details mechanisms for use in controlling a project and informing management of its progress.

The control mechanisms are closely aligned to those of PRINCE with three basic phases to manage:

- project initiation
- main development
- project closure.

Project initiation and project closure procedures are identical to those described for PRINCE. These are primarily the responsibility of the Project Controller. Project initiation may take place before the supply side is involved with the project. If appointed at this time, the Project Manager can provide input to this process to ensure that supply side issues and modes of working are taken into account. The Project Manager can also provide input to planning, based on previous experience in KBS development, especially in respect of technical issues.

The major part of the project is concerned with product development. The main development phase is implemented through the use of the project management process model described in section 4.4.

Main development

Analysis and design products are used to capture the information concerning the system that is being developed. There are eight of these products (models) defined within GEMINI. These models represent the system at varying levels of abstraction. They are not developed in a strict linear fashion, because of their complex interdependence. It must be possible to identify completion criteria for a partial model, if it is to be used in the development of another model. Providing these criteria are properly documented, a partially complete model can be designated a releasable version of a Technical Product. The eight models are detailed in Chapter 8.

There are seven major GEMINI activities for developing the GEMINI Technical Products. Each completed model may be developed by more than one major activity and each major activity may develop more than one model. The major activities are broken down into steps and then tasks, such that a task develops one model or one aspect of a model.

4.4 Project management process model

The *project management process model*, the spiral model, shows how management and control can be imposed on a KBS project, while enabling several development models to be produced in parallel.

4.4.1 Project management process

Each major activity within a project starts with a review when the overall scope of the major activity is defined.

The initial review is followed by a sequence of project management processes:

- risk assessment
- planning
- development
- review.

This sequence of processes is indicated in Figure 4.1 with the main topics for consideration at each point in the sequence.

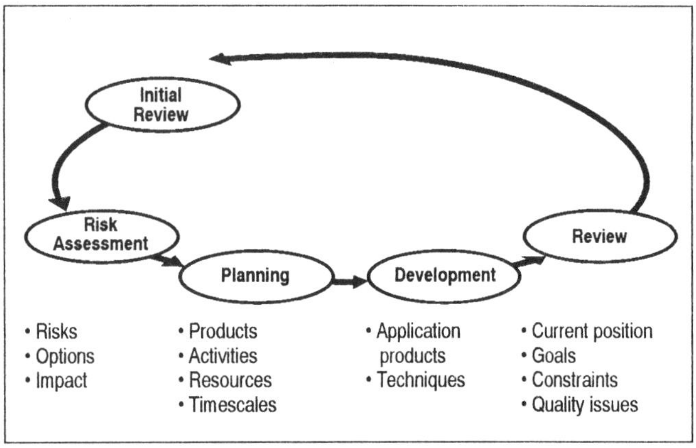

Figure 4.1: The project management processes

The sequence is repeated until all the development activities are complete.

4.4.2 Spiral model

A project is carried out through repetition of the sequence of project management processes. Each iteration of the sequence should yield progress in:

- degree of understanding of outstanding risk
- accuracy of future plans and estimates
- development of the implementable KBS
- quality, that is, assuring the fitness for purpose of products.

The iteration of the project management process sequence can be represented graphically as a spiral. A passage through all four sectors, comprises a circuit of the spiral.

This spiral is illustrated in Figure 4.2.

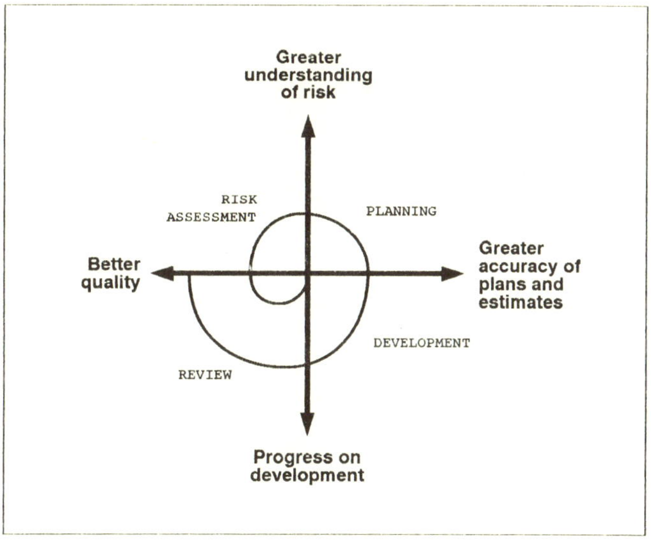

Figure 4.2: Project management process model

The division of the spiral into four sectors does not imply an equal distribution of time or other resources through the sectors.

Initial review

Objectives and constraints are identified during the *initial review* to set the scope for the rest of the spiral. These details must be adequately documented before work covered by the spiral can start.

Risk assessment sector

All major risks are identified or reassessed during the *risk assessment sector.*

All issues which could jeopardise the success of the project need to be considered. An assessment has to be made of impact on the outcome of the project. Resolution options need to be formulated, ramifications identified and their practicality assessed.

Further information on risk assessment procedures is contained in Chapter 6.

Planning sector

During the *planning sector,* the plans are created or adjusted in accordance with changes suggested by the risk assessment and to reflect progress made. This planning may require the update of overall plans as well as the production of detailed technical, resource and quality plans for the activities to be undertaken within the next development sector. Plans should be formulated or adjusted to take account of chosen risk resolution options.

Further information on planning is contained in Chapter 7.

Development sector

The analysis, design and construction activities take place during the *development sector.* This sector will have a longer elapsed time than the other sectors and consume more resources. Its outputs are the Technical Products and progress reports which pass into the review exercise.

Further information on development aspects is contained in Chapter 8.

Review sector

During the *review sector,* the quality and impact of products produced to date are examined and the next set of objectives and constraints identified.

The outputs of the review represent major issues for the other sectors to address.

Review procedures form part of the project quality management. These procedures are documented in section 5.5.

4.4.3 Interpreting the spiral model

A KBS development project can be defined in terms of a set of products which need to be produced. This set of products contains the relevant information on management, quality and technical issues which is required to support a successful project.

Each product identified for a project requires some activity to be undertaken so that it can be developed.

The spiral model relates the management activities of review, risk assessment and planning to the development activities. Each plan and review must be related to the activities and products of the adjacent development sector. It identifies where and how to monitor and control project progress.

Adopting the spiral model helps with the management of the development activities. The required products are identified. These are developed in an appropriate order and manner for resources to be used efficiently and effectively.

A project can be portrayed as an appropriate number of circuits of the spiral as shown in Figure 4.3.

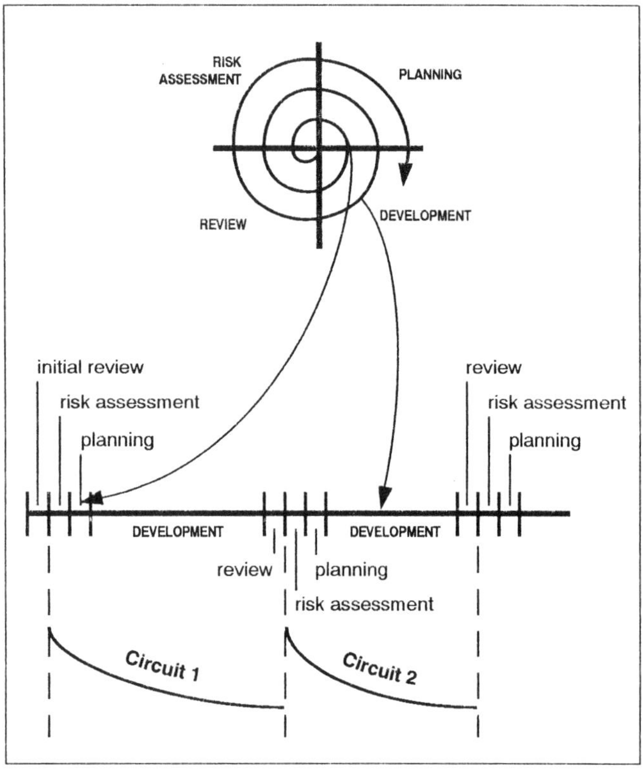

Figure 4.3: A spiral view of a project

Active control by the demand side is mostly exercised during the review, risk assessment and planning sectors. The supply side must advise the Project Controller on the progress of the development activities and any risks or implications identified for the future of the project. The supply side may also need to assess the project and analyse the risks from their own viewpoint.

4.4.4 The hierarchical spiral model

Authority levels and responsibilities are identified in a project and assigned to the various roles in the project. Delegated responsibilities are co-ordinated through the project organisation structure and related directly to the development of products.

The Project Controller is responsible to the Project Board for controlling the delivery of specific major products. In turn, the Project Manager is responsible to the Project Controller for delivering major products.

The Development Team is responsible to the Project Manager for the delivery of certain products. The spiral model can be applied hierarchically, to reflect this organisation hierarchy, as shown in Figure 4.4.

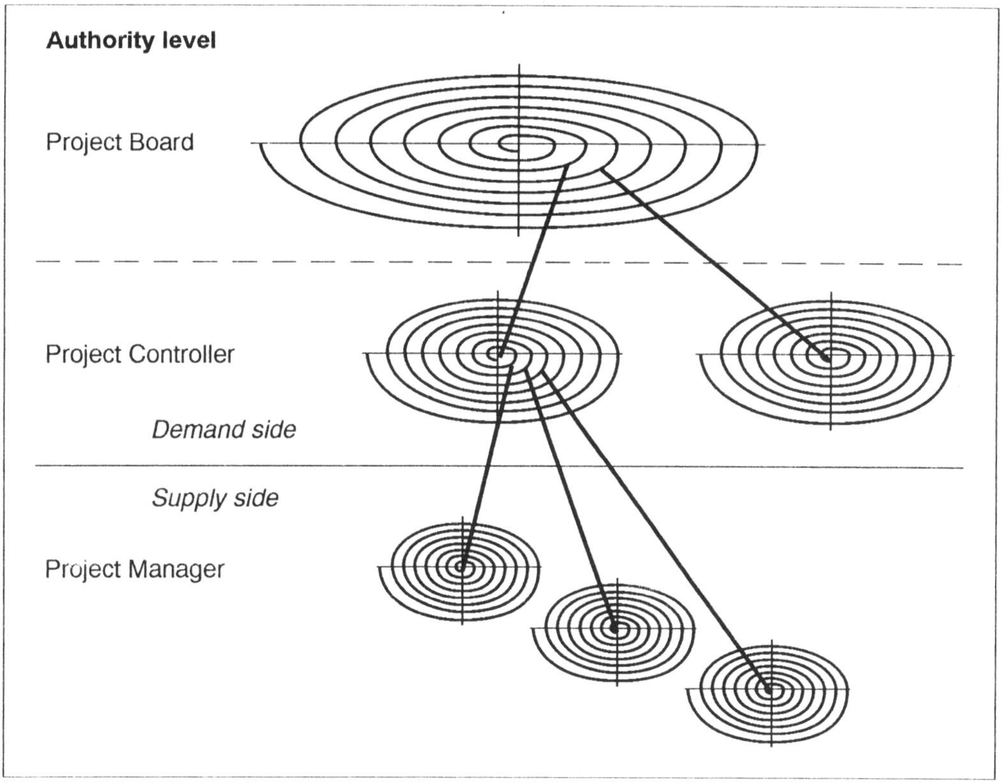

Figure 4.4: A partial hierarchy of spirals

The delegation of responsibilities within the project is reflected in the hierarchy of spirals. The highest-level spiral relates to the whole project and equates to the authority level of the Project Board. The next level relates the activities to develop products and equates to the authority of the Project Controller. The following level reflects the authority of the Project Manager and so on down through the hierarchy.

Several activities may be undertaken concurrently. These activities will be reflected by several spirals operating concurrently.

Spiral interaction

Spirals below the top level are subordinate to higher-level spirals. This relationship is reflected in the interaction between the activities at the different levels. For the lower-level spirals, the:

- risk assessment is likely to be concerned only with the tasks within their scope. The risk assessment at the lower level is subordinate to risk assessment at the parent level. Risks that impact beyond the scope of the spiral in which they are identified must be referred to the parent level
- plans reflect a refinement, but not a modification of part or all of the plan of the parent level
- products are a subset of the products for which the parent is responsible
- review forms input to further review at the parent level.

Levels of authority for resource utilisation will be defined within the project planning exercise. The appropriate level of approval is required before work can be undertaken. This often requires plans to be submitted to the next higher level for approval before development tasks are actually undertaken.

Within each spiral, information relevant to the higher levels is fed up the hierarchy. This information aids monitoring and control and informs decision making at each management level.

4.4.5 Project-level spiral

At the Project Board authority level, control over the whole project is exercised according to the spiral. Each circuit of the spiral equates to a PRINCE stage, or the part of a stage between the end-stage and mid-stage control points. The review, risk assessment and planning sectors of the spiral replace PRINCE mid-stage and end-stage assessments.

The Project Controller is responsible for ensuring that the specified management processes are carried out and for presenting the relevant information to the Project Board for authority to proceed.

At the end of each review sector, the Project Board agree detailed plans for the next risk assessment and planning sectors, together with the scope of the activities in the next development sector.

Each circuit of this spiral is concerned with:

- assessing project progress against high-level plans
- managing risks to the success of the project
- setting project objectives in terms of major deliverables
- planning the work to develop deliverables
- assessing the quality of deliverables
- controlling and managing budgets.

This spiral is controlled by the Project Board using information provided by the Project Controller.

4.4.6 Second-level spirals

The Project Controller will create a second-level spiral for each major activity of the project (see 7.4.6) before the activity starts. Since activities may be carried out concurrently, several of these spirals may be operative at any time. Each second-level spiral consists of an initial review followed by the cycle of risk assessment, planning, development and review. The spirals are subordinate to the project-level spiral and must be co-ordinated with it. The Project Controller exercises authority at the second level and gives approval for each spiral circuit from documentation presented by the Project Manager.

The Project Controller deals with issues within the Project Controller's assigned authority level and reports any project-level issues to the Project Board, using the prescribed mechanisms for monitoring and control.

During the development sector, the Project Controller needs to liaise with the Project Manager to keep abreast of progress and ensure that relevant issues are addressed. This liaison involves the use of established mechanisms for regular progress reports, relevant to the demand side, from the Project Manager including any exceptions or risks identified.

4.4.7 Lower-level spirals

At each lower level within the project, activities for each spiral start with an initial review followed by a cycle of risk assessment, planning, development and review. During each spiral, activities may be divided into sub-activities, each of which may be controlled in the same manner as the parent level with its own smaller cycle of risk assessment, planning, development and review.

Spirals below the second level must be controlled by the Project Manager. These spirals feed information to the higher-level spirals. The depth and number of spirals should be set as appropriate. Responsibility for some spirals may be delegated to Team Leaders. The Development Team should be encouraged to use spiral model concepts for tasks too small to be controlled using a documented spiral.

4.5 Spiral co-ordination

Each lower-level spiral relates to one or more circuits of the parent spiral, and develops a defined product or set of products. Lower-level spirals develop products which form components of the product set of the parent spiral and are instigated, as appropriate, during a parent-level spiral planning sector.

Several spirals may operate concurrently using resources delegated from the parent spiral. The parent spiral needs information on progress, resource usage, risks and plans from these lower spirals during the review, risk assessment and planning sectors.

Spirals must be organised so that information is available to the parent spiral at the appropriate time. Any significant issues that arise at control points are passed up using appropriate PRINCE mechanisms.

4.6 Summary

The Project Manager should ensure that the supply side aspects of the project are managed according to the project management process model. This emphasises the need for regular risk assessment, planning and review.

Progress reports must be produced as an input to those reviews for which the Project Controller has responsibility.

Any risks identified by the Project Manager or Development Team which impact the project should be reported to the Project Controller.

Appropriate planning information should be passed to the Project Controller as input to plans for the next set of development activities.

5 Project quality management

5.1 Introduction

Quality is defined in ISO 8402 as:

> *the totality of features and characteristics of a product or service that bear on its ability to satisfy stated or implied needs.*

Organisations wishing to achieve efficiency and effectiveness by managing quality must develop policies, processes and systems which ensure that all activities under their control are aligned to their business needs.

Project management forms an important part of any organisation's overall quality management. Further information on quality can be found in the Quality Management Library. This chapter discusses quality management within the context of a GEMINI project.

Although quality should permeate all aspects of the project, specific activities to ensure quality are concentrated largely within the review sector of the project management process model. The activities carried out during risk assessment sectors and planning sectors contribute substantially to enabling development sector activities to deliver quality products.

The policies and processes governing quality aspects of a GEMINI project will be those of the demand side. The supply side must convince the demand side, before the project starts, of their ability and willingness to adhere to any quality requirements.

This Chapter gives a context for quality management on a GEMINI project and specific guidance on the Project Manager's responsibilities.

5.1.1 Quality management concepts

Successful application of quality management requires that there is a quality management framework with a supporting quality infrastructure in order to develop quality products and services in an efficient and effective manner. The quality management framework defines the policies and practices for managing quality. Quality management in terms of projects assures and controls development activities through the use of various techniques, including reviews, walkthroughs and inspections. Systematic processes are used and documented for project management, project execution and project control.

Project quality management must operate within any quality management framework of the demand side organisation.

Quality in this chapter is considered under:

- quality assurance (section 5.2)
- quality control (section 5.3)
- documentation for quality (section 5.4)
- quality and the review sector (section 5.5)
- configuration management (section 5.6).

5.1.2 Quality issues

Typical concerns for quality include:

- delivery on time within budget
- ensuring that the developed products satisfy the defined requirements within the given constraints
- checking that the quality processes are being followed correctly
- maintaining accurate records of the development process
- maintaining accurate records of versions of products
- correcting faults in the quality processes
- improving quality processes.

The aim of addressing these concerns is to achieve project objectives efficiently and effectively. Good communications are required to ensure that all members of the project organisation follow the prescribed quality management approach.

5.1.3 Quality issues for knowledge based systems

Achieving quality in knowledge based systems presents challenges which must be addressed. These challenges include:

- controlling parallel development
- checking outputs produced iteratively
- checking partially completed products
- uncertainty about the knowledge to be captured, its applicability and use
- validating knowledge based specifications.

The first three points are addressed through use of the project management process model and rigorous configuration management (see section 5.6). The fourth point is addressed by risk assessment, the flexible approach and iterative development. The last point needs to be considered as part of the quality control procedures (see section 5.3).

The origin of information which is to be incorporated within the KBS must be identified. Records of information origin and transformation form an important part of the auditability of the KBS development and operation.

During the development phase, consideration should be given to the implications of future maintainability on the development. This may affect the requirements for the documentation of products and for the associated development processes.

Adopting suitable quality management processes minimises risks to the project's effective and efficient completion.

5.2 Quality assurance

Quality assurance (QA) as described in ISO 8402 - 1986 covers:

> *all those planned and systematic actions that provide adequate confidence that a product or service will satisfy given requirements for quality.*

QA techniques involve:

- planning for quality
- specifying cost-effective quality control processes
- reviewing the quality control practice eg. through audits
- using feedback to improve quality control processes.

Everyone involved in a project must develop products to stated requirements. Adoption of quality assurance techniques is a signal that quality is being built into the project products.

The quality assurance processes for a project must be agreed at project initiation. The processes will build on the demand side organisation's existing quality management framework and standards, taking into account project specific requirements.

The supply side will have its own quality standards and quality management systems, which may be applicable to a GEMINI project. However, the Project Manager must satisfy the Project Controller that the supply side employs quality assurance processes which are compatible with the requirements of the project. During negotiations, the Project Manager must provide information to the Project Controller to establish that the methods and communications proposed by the supply side will ensure conformance to demand side quality policies and standards.

There is a wide choice of methods, systems and techniques available to support quality management. A number of generic quality standards including ISO 9001 are in wide use.

Information on supply side compliance with standards, and details of any accreditation, will be required by the Project Controller.

5.2.1 Roles and quality assurance

The *Project Board* has ultimate responsibility for project quality. Monitoring and controlling quality processes is delegated to the Project Controller who is supported in this by the:

- Project Manager
- Project Assurance Team
- Configuration Librarian.

Every member of the project organisation carries some responsibility for quality. Commitment to quality throughout the project organisation is essential. Personnel should be encouraged and motivated to seek cost-effective improvements which benefit the demand organisation.

Project Controller

The *Project Controller* is responsible for ensuring that the project meets its quality objectives within the agreed timescales and budgets. The Project Controller will make explicit what is required to enable the quality requirements to be met. The basic approach to achieving quality is documented in the quality assurance statement (QAS) described in section 5.4.

The Project Controller ensures that the defined quality approach is followed, by specifying controls in plans and quality criteria in product descriptions.

Project Manager

The *Project Manager* must satisfy the Project Controller that an appropriate approach to quality is followed by the supply side. This approach must ensure that the supply side meets the objectives for quality set by the demand side.

The Project Manager provides information to the Project Controller for inclusion in quality plans. This information includes identifying activities and resources required to develop products and appropriate quality criteria.

The Project Manager must carry out a number of tasks to ensure that the required quality is achieved, including:

- agreeing quality and technical approaches with the Project Controller
- communicating quality requirements to the Development Team and ensuring conformance with the QAS
- ensuring that all the supply side roles on the organisational structure are assigned to competent individuals with the requisite skills and knowledge
- monitoring quality processes within the development activities
- liaison with the Project Controller on quality issues
- monitoring and controlling the resources within supply side responsibilities
- monitoring progress against plans
- informing the Project Controller of any risks to quality that are identified.

The Project Manager may also have separate responsibility for quality management within any supply side project to control the work.

Project Assurance Team (PAT)

The *Project Assurance Team* is responsible for ensuring that adequate quality assurance and control are undertaken. The PAT does not necessarily undertake these functions itself but monitors that the processes built into the project activities deliver quality products and, if necessary, propose improvements to these processes.

Configuration Librarian

Products are developed for each project and many will be subject to change during the life of the project. Configuration management (see 5.6) is used to ensure that changes to products are correctly applied and documented. The *Configuration Librarian* is responsible for planning, monitoring and reporting on all configuration management aspects of the project.

5.3 Quality control

Quality control encompasses the operational techniques and activities for use in satisfying project and product requirements. These techniques and activities ensure that:

- quality criteria are specified for all products
- required qualities are built into products
- defects in products are detected and removed
- defects in the production and control processes are identified and corrected
- progress is monitored against planned timescales and resource usage.

Quality control activities are mainly carried out in the review sector of the spiral. These activities encompass:

- reviewing products
- testing products
- inspecting products
- auditing production processes
- reviewing processes
- monitoring progress
- measuring resource usage.

Product quality

The criteria to which each developed product must conform is defined by the Project Controller as part of the product description. Any defects in a product must be detected and removed unless explicitly allowed by the Project Board.

Quality criteria in product descriptions document the quality requirements for each product. Quality criteria are the characteristics associated with a product. These criteria are used to determine whether the product meets requirements and, thus, define quality in the context of the product. Quality criteria must be applied to the product during development and will be used by the demand side to assess compliance.

Quality control processes must ensure traceability of products. They must provide the ability to trace the history, application or location of an item. It is impossible to ensure quality without traceability.

In software development, a number of specific activities may be carried out as part of the process of detecting defects including inspection, reviews, checking and testing. The importance of quality control procedures is emphasised within GEMINI by the review sector of the spiral (see 5.5).

Production process quality

Progress of the project and development of products must be monitored and compared to that planned including completion dates. Use of manpower, skills, money, equipment and other resources are checked against plans for progress made.

Part of the quality control process is to monitor the efficiency and effectiveness of the production and control processes. This includes identifying defects in the processes and non-conformance to the quality assurance statement. Weaknesses must be documented and a report passed to the level of management which has the responsibility for defining and enforcing suitable action for rectification.

5.4 Documentation for quality

Documentation on a project provides a record of activities and their results. It ranges from a record of what was agreed at meetings to specifications of the demand side requirements and the other products of the development process.

GEMINI defines two types of complementary documents to prescribe the two facets of quality planning on a project. These documents are the:

- quality assurance statement (QAS)
- quality plan.

5.4.1 Quality assurance statement

The *quality assurance statement* (QAS) documents the quality approach for the project. It is developed by the Project Controller to specify quality issues which must be addressed throughout the project.

The approach is defined and documented at project initiation. This statement is referenced from, or included in, the Project Initiation Document.

If the approach for quality needs to be amended during the project, the quality assurance statement will be revised by the Project Controller and approved by the Project Board.

The QAS covers:

- identification of quality processes for the project including references to applicable policies, codes of practice and standards
- determination of overall quality requirements for products and development activities, including formats, methods and applicable standards
- identification of the control mechanisms to be used in the project to ensure the quality of products and control the use of resources, including metrics, reporting lines, reporting procedures and review procedures
- mechanisms for review and improvement of the quality processes for the project to ensure it fulfils its objectives.

The Project Controller has overall responsibility for preparation of the QAS and ensuring compliance with its provisions. The Project Manager may be required to provide input to the QAS and must ensure supply side conformance with its provisions.

5.4.2 Quality plan

Every plan within GEMINI includes a quality plan, which documents the quality requirements for the products and activities covered by that plan. A quality plan defines the:

- quality control processes specific to the products and activities covered by the plan
- timetable of major review activities
- list of review participants and their role in the review
- procedures and methods for the review

- products covered by the plan and a reference to the product description for each product
- details of how the breakdown of products is to be used for configuration management purposes.

Each quality plan references the relevant part of the current QAS and gives any additional detail required for the operation of quality controls within the remit of the plan.

Product descriptions are produced as part of the technical plans and each contains the purpose of a product, a definition of its content and quality criteria. Products must be developed according to their product descriptions which are used to assess fitness for purpose of the developed product.

A set of skeleton product descriptions for an exemplar GEMINI project are given in Chapter 5 of the volume *GEMINI Technical Reference.* Product descriptions of particular relevance to the Project Manager are in Annex C of the current volume.

Assessing fitness for purpose involves validating that the product conforms to the product description. There are a variety of techniques which can be used for validations, some of which relate directly to validation of KBS products. Additional information on techniques is found in the volume *GEMINI Technical Reference.*

Quality plans will detail how testing will be carried out and detail roles and responsibilities for verification and testing. There are likely to be tests of individual components of the KBS. As these components are built into the whole system, additional checks are needed to ensure that the interfaces between components operate as predicted.

5.4.3 Quality agreement

The Project Manager provides technical details of the work to be undertaken by the supply side, as input to planning and quality plans. The Project Controller will ensure that the plans conform to the objectives and policy laid down in the QAS.

Detailed quality requirements to be met by the supply side must be agreed with the demand side and form part of any formal agreement for delivery of products or services.

5.5 Quality and the review sector

The project management process model emphasises the importance of quality control activities by incorporating a review sector.

The initial review of the project-level spiral sets overall objectives for the project and is documented in the quality assurance statement within the PID.

During subsequent review sectors, quality is controlled by:

- monitoring progress against plans
- reviewing processes and identifying problems
- reviewing products of the current circuit of the spiral (see 5.5.1)
- setting quality objectives and constraints for the next circuit of the spiral (see 5.5.2).

The outputs from the review sector form major issues to be addressed within other sectors of the spiral.

5.5.1 Reviewing products

The purpose of a product quality review is to assess the product's conformance to the stated specification.

The product originator must review a product during its development but may be too involved to judge fitness for purpose objectively. It is necessary to have a mechanism to allow an independent review of the product. The product quality review allows for input from both project and non-project staff who can apply relevant experience and knowledge to the task.

A product quality review involves checking the product against quality criteria set out in the product description. Some areas for consideration in the review are:

- format and content of the product
- correct use of the source documents specified in the product description
- deviations from standards specified in the product description
- completeness
- consistency
- suitability for intended purpose.

The supply side must carry out its own reviews of products produced by the Project Manager and Development Team. Deliverables must then be submitted to the Project Controller for demand side review. A list of any identified errors will be compiled to check that corrections are applied.

Correction of major deficiencies may be carried out in a subordinate spiral which must:

- assess the risks involved in making a correction, that is, the effect on resources and schedules, or in not making a correction, that is, the effect on fulfilling requirements [risk assessment sector]
- plan the activities and resources needed to correct the deficiency [planning sector]
- modify the product to correct the deficiency [development sector]
- check that the deficiency has been corrected [review sector].

Errors which cannot be addressed satisfactorily must be documented so that further action can be planned.

5.5.2 The next circuit of the spiral

During the review sectors of top-level and second-level spirals, as well as looking back over the current circuit of the spiral, the Project Controller considers the next circuit. This is the point where the way forward is clarified. In an ideal situation, just additional detail is required. More commonly project objectives need to be revisited and some adjustment of direction is required.

The review sector provides detail for the next risk assessment and planning sectors together with the scope of the next development sector. By the end of review, the orientation is set for the next circuit of the spiral.

Risk assessment

Any risks likely to impact on the quality of the products or activities for the project should be identified. All risks identified during the review sector will be documented as input to the risk assessment activities.

Planning

Any change of direction, amendment to project objectives, changes of estimates or refinement of understanding should be documented as input to the planning sector.

5.6 Configuration management

Configuration management is controlled by the Configuration Librarian and is a set of techniques and procedures to record, monitor and control the status of pre-defined items which must be developed through the lifetime of the project.

Configuration management can be broken down into four parts:

- identification and definition of items
- controlling changes to items throughout the project
- recording and monitoring the status of items
- providing traceability of the items.

Configuration Management of deliverables is a demand side responsibility but may require information and support from the Project Manager and any supply side Configuration Librarian. Information which may be provided by the supply side includes:

- those components of a deliverable which may be used independently
- what activities create each component of each deliverable
- what activities use each component of each deliverable
- the interaction in use of components and their deliverables.

5.7 Summary

This chapter provides guidance on the various quality activities including quality assurance, quality control and configuration management, within the context of a KBS development project. These activities have been briefly explained. Quality management applies to projects for the development of conventional systems. The techniques required for KBS do not differ greatly, though generally require more stringent controls to be applied.

Everyone is responsible for quality

It is important to monitor the quality of products and procedures. All members of the project organisation must be part of a culture which encourages the use of a common quality approach to project activities and seek continuous improvements.

Project Manager and quality

The Project Manager provides the interface between the Project Controller and the Development Team.

The Project Manager has responsibility for ensuring that the Development Team conforms to the demand side quality policies, and must be prepared to satisfy the Project Controller on this.

6 Risk management

6.1 Introduction

This chapter deals with the issues that arise in the management of risk in a KBS development project.

In a project, *risk* is the likelihood and impact of that project failing to:

- meet a business need and provide the expected business benefits
- prove technically feasible
- prove organisationally feasible
- be completed on time and within budget
- develop products which meet requirements.

The emphasis in GEMINI on risk management is highlighted by having a sector of the spiral model dedicated to risk assessment.

At the overall project-level (top-level spiral), risk management is carried out through the implementation of Project Board decisions in respect of identified risks. The Project Controller identifies risks to the Project Board and provides information to facilitate this decision making.

At lower levels of the spiral hierarchy the processes of risk management will be broadly similar. However, the formality with which risk assessment is carried out and the allocation of responsibilities vary considerably according to the level concerned.

Action, to address the risks identified, is taken in the planning and development sectors. The success of this action is assessed in the review sector.

The Project Manager must provide the Project Controller with information concerning risks associated with the development and implementation of the KBS. The Project Manager may also have responsibility to provide information concerning risks to any supply side Project Board.

More information on risk management from the demand side perspective can be found in the publication *GEMINI: Controlling KBS Development Projects*.

6.1.1 Risk management

Risk management is the process by which the risks to, and inherent in, a project are identified, understood, analysed and addressed. The assumptions on which a project plan is based need to be questioned in order to identify risks, evaluate different risk resolution options and enable informed decisions to be taken on those options. Risk management includes the ongoing review of all aspects of project feasibility.

It is not risk which is detrimental to the outcome of a project, but failure to identify a risk and either prevent its manifestation or mitigate any potential damage. The Project Controller is responsible to the Project Board for risk management. The Project Manager must ensure that all reasonable steps are taken by the supply side to manage the risks to a project effectively and efficiently. Fulfilling this responsibility involves managing the risks within the supply side remit and maintaining the Project Controller's awareness of the risks and of how they are to be resolved. Any risks identified by the supply side which have implications for the demand side or require demand side action should be documented and reported to the Project Controller.

6.1.2 When risk management occurs

Risks pose threats throughout a project's lifetime, so risk management must occur throughout the project. The processes of identification and analysis of risk occur primarily in the risk assessment sector of the spiral. Some risks may have been identified during the review sector. The options chosen to control the risks may affect the plans and form inputs to the planning sector. Any risks identified during the development sector should be documented for inclusion in the next review, unless they warrant an exception report.

6.2 Risks specific to KBS developments

The management of risk in KBS projects has strong parallels with that in conventional developments. However, emphasis is placed on the need to manage risk in KBS projects because of the particular attributes of these projects. Some significant attributes are that:

- the processes of knowledge acquisition and knowledge representation are not widely understood
- the requirements specification is often less well defined and more volatile than for conventional systems
- the Expert may find it difficult and may sometimes be unwilling to explain all the relevant knowledge in a way that the Knowledge Engineer can understand. The Expert may be advising on problems to which there is no single, correct answer
- the development process tends to be more iterative than for conventional systems
- there is no large body of metrics on past KBS developments to enable reasonable estimates of development and implementation costs to be made
- KBSs may incorporate subjective or imprecise information
- KBSs are often highly interactive systems

- validation tends to be difficult to scope as KBS usually contain more complex logic than conventional systems. Testing often requires an extensive range of cases together with acceptable solutions to each case
- there are sometimes problems over organisational issues such as job security, de-skilling, demarcation and security of proprietary knowledge
- many operational KBSs require frequent changes to the knowledge and rules that they use. This requires in-built flexibility to facilitate maintenance and enhancement
- users sometimes misunderstand the power and limitations of systems which appear to be able to analyse and reason.

6.3 The risk assessment process

Because knowledge based systems are more prone to risks than conventional systems GEMINI advocates an explicit risk assessment activity following each review.

All risk assessments involve a number of specific tasks. including:

- risk identification
- risk quantification
- identification of resolution options.

Risk identification

Risk identification addresses the problems of whether the delivery of any product to the demand side is at risk for business, technical, organisational or external reasons and what the individual risks are.

Risk quantification

It is important to appreciate that there are two dimensions to the seriousness of risk:

- *probability*, which is a measure of the likelihood that each risk will materialise and impact the project negatively
- *severity*, which is a measure of the expected extent of such negative impact.

Both dimensions are used to form a single assessment of the seriousness of each risk. This seriousness may vary over time, requiring the risks to be regularly reassessed.

Resolution option identification

The most serious risks are analysed and possible options for reducing the seriousness of each of these risks are identified. Each option may affect a risk's probability, severity or both.

Project Manager's role

The Project Manager must ensure that these tasks are carried out within the supply side area of responsibility. Information must be provided to the Project Controller for risk management to be carried out within the demand side level of responsibility.

The Project Manager is responsible for ensuring that the right level of information is collected by the supply side and passed to the Project Controller.

6.4 Legal aspects of risk

Actions taken by any party, which are governed by enforceable regulations or might affect another party, will have legal implications. Any transaction between parties has potential legal implications. These legal implications may give rise to specific risks to a project from legal proceedings.

The Project Manager is responsible for representing the supply side interests in any contractual negotiations with the Project Controller. During the course of a project the Project Manager should ensure that the Development Team does not take any action that puts the demand side at legal risk and alert the Project Controller to any legal issues that become apparent.

6.4.1 Constraints

There are national laws and regulations governing many of the activities that may be undertaken in the course of a KBS development project.

As well as national ones, where a project has a foreign dimension, it may also be necessary to take account of:

- international laws and regulations imposed by binding treaties and conventions
- supranational laws and regulations imposed by a supranational entity such as the EC
- foreign national laws and regulations.

European Community Directives and GATT Government Procurement Agreements are extremely important to procurement activity within the public sector.

6.4.2 Obligations

Each of the parties to any agreement assumes obligations to the other. These obligations may be in terms of:

- performance of agreed actions
- provision of agreed goods or services
- payment of agreed sums
- taking care to prevent damage to persons or property.

The parties will have obligations to third parties where their actions may have an impact on such third parties.

Failure to exercise care over actions affecting another party may result in some harm or loss. This is the area most affected by the multiplicity of parties typically involved in KBS projects. There are a variety of parties who may be affected by the operation of a KBS either directly, by taking its advice, or indirectly, by action taken as a result of such advice. There are a variety of parties involved in the production and operation of a KBS:

- experts
- Knowledge Engineers
- operators/IT service providers
- maintainers
- users.

Apportionment of responsibility in the event of a claim for damages is likely to be complex unless there is a clear audit trail of the source of the knowledge and the ways that it has been transformed, used and maintained.

6.4.3 Ownership rights

There are types of property which can be owned and ownership can pass from one party to another.

A legal category of intangible property which is particularly significant in system development is *intellectual property*. The principal types of rights in intellectual property are *patent, copyright, trademarks* and *confidentiality*. It is possible to secure these rights individually.

Where a formal contract governs the supply/demand side relationship, it is important that any ownership rights are clearly documented.

6.4.4 Liabilities

If a legal obligation is not met or a constraint is broken, then the party committing the breach may find itself liable to pay:

- fines for breach of formal regulations. For example, those relating to the misuse of computers, the processing of personal information or the use of telecommunications
- damages for particular acts or omissions. For example, failure to take sufficient care in constructing a system, or any part of it, when that failure causes reasonably foreseeable loss or injury
- compensation for breach of an agreement between parties. For example, failing to perform some agreed action.

In law, liability may exist where professional advice has caused economic loss in a situation where it is reasonable for the claimant to have relied on the special expertise of the adviser.

6.5 Summary

The Project Manager must be able to show that risk management forms an integral part of the development process. Information relating to project risks must be given to the Project Controller, who, for the demand side, has the responsibility of ensuring that risk is managed throughout the project.

There may be KBS specific expertise on the supply side, which is useful to the Project Controller in all aspects of risk management. The Project Manager should liaise with the Project Controller on all aspects of risk management throughout the project.

A particular category of risk, which should exercise minds on both supply and demand sides, is legal risk. In cases where there is any doubt or conflict about legal obligations and liabilities, expert assistance should be sought.

7 Planning

7.1 Introduction

The same detailed planning mechanisms can be used on a GEMINI project as are used in connection with conventional IS development projects. GEMINI planning differs from PRINCE planning, however, by fitting planning to the spiral model and also on account of differences in the following:

- planning documentation
- products developed in the project
- applicable techniques.

This chapter concentrates on the planning issues specific to GEMINI projects and provides guidance for producing and reviewing plans. A plan must focus on the development of required products, which means that it must cover the resourcing and scheduling of an appropriate set of activities.

7.1.1 Planning concepts

Planning is the process of estimating, collating, sequencing and scheduling the project's resources to deliver the required products. It involves identifying activities to develop the right products, in the right way, at the right time, at the right cost and in the right order.

Plan

A *plan* documents the results of the planning process. It shows targets in terms of products, timescales, costs and quality. It shows how the identified resources have been scheduled to meet these targets.

Estimating

An *estimate* is an assessment of the size of the task in terms of required resources, cost and timescale. Estimates should be refined as the project proceeds.

7.1.2 When to plan

An outline Project Plan, defining major products and the activity schedule for the project, is produced at project initiation and forms part of the Project Initiation Document. This plan forms a baseline which is referenced throughout the project to monitor progress.

From the second circuit onwards, initial planning for individual circuits of the spiral is carried out at the end of the review sector for the preceding circuit and documented in the Circuit Initiation Document (CID). A CID is similar to a Project Initiation Document, but has a narrower focus and contains more detail. A CID contains documentation of detailed planning for the risk assessment and planning sectors of the spiral and sets the scope for the development and review sectors.

The detailed plans for development and review processes are produced in the planning sector and documented in Development Sector Plans.

Planning takes place in lower-level spirals in a similar way. The documentation produced will be appropriate to the level of the particular spiral.

7.2 Planning issues

All identified activities must conform to the project's terms of reference as laid down in the Project Initiation Document.

It is important to allocate resources to all the activities needed in all the sectors of the spiral model. Most resources will be consumed within the development sector. This does not mean that review, risk assessment and planning are not important, simply that these sectors are used to monitor and focus the development effort. The products of the review and risk assessment sectors provide input to the planning sector.

The products of KBS development projects are generally closely related and some need to be developed in parallel. Care needs to be taken to identify dependencies and highlight them within the plans. The spiral hierarchy can help to control this type of development.

Planning involves scheduling *estimated* resources and it is unlikely that actual usage will match estimates exactly. Project Boards normally agree a level of tolerance which can be allowed for the whole project and allocate this across parts of the project. There is no comprehensive body of metrics for KBS development projects, to aid the estimating process. The supply side may be expected to provide input on the basis of previous experience on KBS development projects.

7.3 Structure and types of plan

Plans are produced at several levels in a project. The structure of each plan is similar but the coverage varies.

The Project Plan should contain a high-level description of the activities to be undertaken to generate all the required products for complete analysis and design of the proposed system. Other plans focus in more detail on the products and activities of parts of the project.

A plan generally includes some narrative of what is detailed and an explanation of reasons for inclusion or exclusion of activities.

7.3.1 Structure of plans

There are three aspects to all GEMINI plans which are documented to form a complete picture. These aspects reflect the major considerations of the planning process:

- *technical* which describes what products should be produced when
- *resource* which details and schedules resources required to carry out the development activities
- *quality* which describes how quality issues should be addressed throughout the activities.

In PRINCE, quality planning is documented within the technical and resource plans. GEMINI makes the quality plans explicit to emphasise the importance of quality planning.

There is a product description for plans in Annex C.

Technical plan

A *technical plan* shows the products to be developed and target completion dates with agreed tolerances. Individuals, their roles and involvement are identified.

The technical plan within the Project Plan shows the circuits of the top-level spiral for the full project and the major products to be developed in each circuit. Dependencies between the project and other projects should be identified.

Resource plan

A *resource plan* includes estimates of the amount of each resource type required during each time period. These estimates should be based on the detail in the technical and quality plans.

A resource plan includes the resourcing requirements for each activity, including any tolerance allowed.

Quality plan

A *quality plan* includes details of quality processes, including product reviews, frequency of checkpoint meetings and Highlight Report production. Quality plans are based on the quality assurance statement in the PID or current CID. Where possible, names of reviewers are identified.

7.3.2 Types of plan

All plans cover the issues of technical, resource and quality planning. Within GEMINI, several types of plan are identified; these become more detailed as they refer to smaller blocks of work. Figure 7.1 shows the types of plan identified.

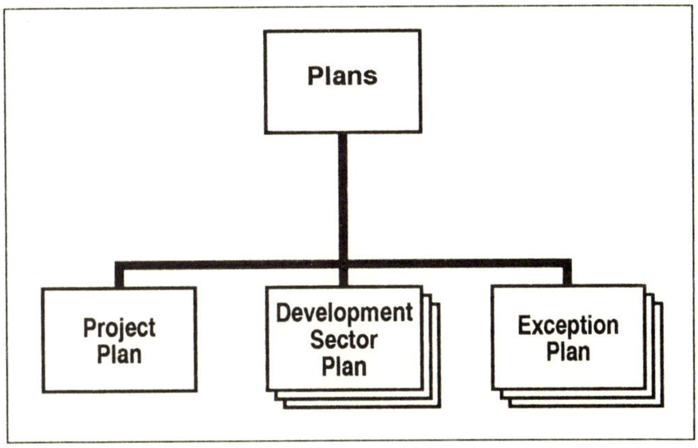

Figure 7.1: Types of plan

Project Plan

The Project Plan sets out the overall approach which is to be taken on the project. The products and activities covered will be major ones.

The Project Plan is a management tool for monitoring progress and a means of communication between Project Board, Project Controller and Project Manager. The document shows which products are to be developed and delivered from the supply side to the demand side and the associated activities for the project concerned.

Development Sector Plan

Each circuit of the spiral is focused on the production of a set of products; their development must be planned in detail. For each set of Technical Products, the work is undertaken in the development sector.

Development Sector Plans document and schedule the resources required to develop the products covered by the current circuit of the spiral.

Development Sector Plans, as all GEMINI plans, have technical, resource and quality elements.

Exception Plan

An Exception Plan documents an unplanned situation which has arisen, or is likely to arise, and records the proposed corrective action. Possible options for addressing the situation are documented as part of this type of plan.

GEMINI Exception Plans are produced and used in exactly the same way as in PRINCE. The only difference is the separation of quality elements.

7.4 Development activities

The development sector is the most resource intensive of the spiral sectors. The activities of other sectors are carried out to ensure that the development activities deliver the required products effectively, efficiently and economically.

Development Sector Plans cover the products to be developed in the current spiral circuit and the activities to develop those products.

Planning is carried out to ensure that the project organisation, and in particular the Development Team:

- develop the right products
- develop the products in the right sequence, taking account of dependencies
- review the products in the right way at the right time
- utilise the right inputs
- involve the right participants at the right time.

Plans form a particularly important aspect of the documentation between demand and supply sides. Plans detail what has to be developed when, and with what resources. They may be used by the demand side to compare achievements against those planned, as input to assessments of supply side performance.

The Project Manager needs to ensure that the plans adequately reflect the supply side activities required to develop the products concerned before accepting the plans.

7.4.1 Required products

A set of development products is described in Chapter 8. Production of these products can be scheduled in a diagram to identify the dependencies between products and activities.

Development of products may be under direct supply side control. The format of deliverables and timescales, and the resources needed to develop them, form part of the plans. The Project Manager must agree these with the Project Controller.

The Project Manager must satisfy the Project Controller of the appropriateness of activities to be used to develop products.

7.4.2 Product dependencies

To identify and plan project activities, the contents of the products to be developed and the dependencies between products need to be understood.

Development of one product may depend on the availability of other products or external inputs. Dependencies between example GEMINI products are represented in Figure 7.2.

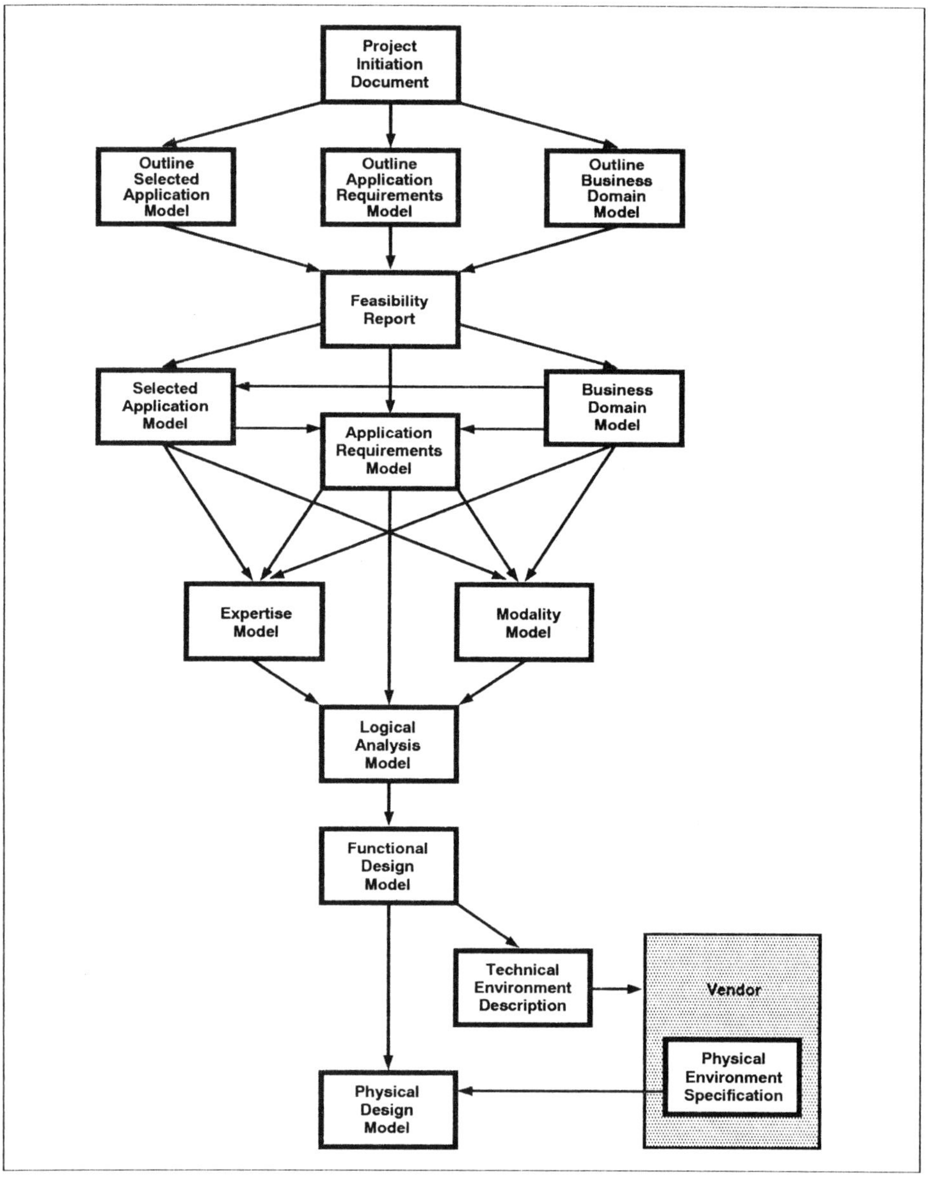

Figure 7.2: Simplified Product Flow Diagram

The most complex interdependencies in a KBS project are between the models which represent the transformation from requirements to implementable system. It is possible to work on models in parallel provided the logical interdependencies allow it and provided there are completeness criteria identified to allow an assessment of the state of completion of a model. Various states of completeness of a range of models are illustrated in Figure 7.3.

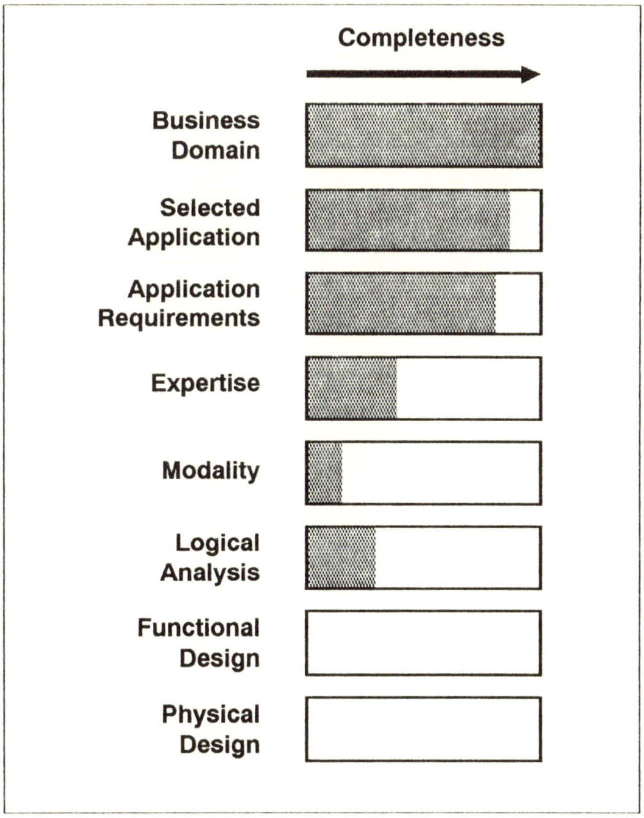

Figure 7.3: Various states of completeness of the key GEMINI development models

An incomplete model developed to predefined criteria is a discrete Technical Product. Where one model depends on another, it is not possible to fully complete the former before completion of the latter. Planning for any project needs to determine the products required. An exemplar set of GEMINI products and development activities is described in the volume *GEMINI Technical Reference*. For any particular KBS development, the Technical Products may be a subset of the exemplar GEMINI products or may include additional products.

7.4.3 Product Reviews

A product review takes place towards the end of each development sector. This review is used by the supply side to check the quality of the Technical Products of the sector and to identify any additional work required.

The demand side must be able to make sure that products are delivered to the required quality. Products will be assessed for fitness for purpose and the documented results input to the review of project progress, as part of the following review sector. The Project Manager must plan supply side product reviews, either involving the Project Controller or providing reports as input to the review sector. Where the product is a deliverable, the demand side may carry out formal acceptance testing.

7.4.4 Relevant inputs

All inputs to an activity to develop products must be identified and defined. Most inputs have been developed as Technical Products of the project. The planning process is used to identify which inputs are required to start a development activity and then to schedule activities to ensure that they are available when required.

Any activity may require inputs which are products of other activities within the project. An activity should not be initiated until all products required for the activity have been developed to a sufficient level of detail. The inter-dependence of products means that some activities can be performed concurrently, while others must be sequential.

7.4.5 Relevant participants

Specific skills and knowledge are required both to generate and to review Technical Products. All participants in these activities and their availability must be identified and scheduled. For the development models, participants are mainly Knowledge Engineers, Users, Experts and Configuration Librarians.

7.4.6 GEMINI major activities

All projects need to be broken down into manageable parts. Each of these parts that develops important products is a *major activity*.

The work to be carried out in a GEMINI project has been grouped into the following major activities:

Activity FS	Feasibility Study
Activity RA	Requirements Analysis
Activity SM	System Modelling
Activity LA	Logical Analysis
Activity LD	Logical Design
Activity TE	Technical Environment Definition
Activity PD	Physical Design

These activities need to be tailored to fit the circumstances of each individual project.

In order to create detailed plans, work structures should be constructed for all major activities.

7.4.7 Diagram notation

It is important to understand the notation used in GEMINI in order to follow its diagrams. GEMINI uses work structures to represent the inter-relationships between activities and the intermediate and project products they generate.

Figure 7.4 illustrates the notation used for a GEMINI work structure. There are three components representing:

- activities
- products
- product/information flows.

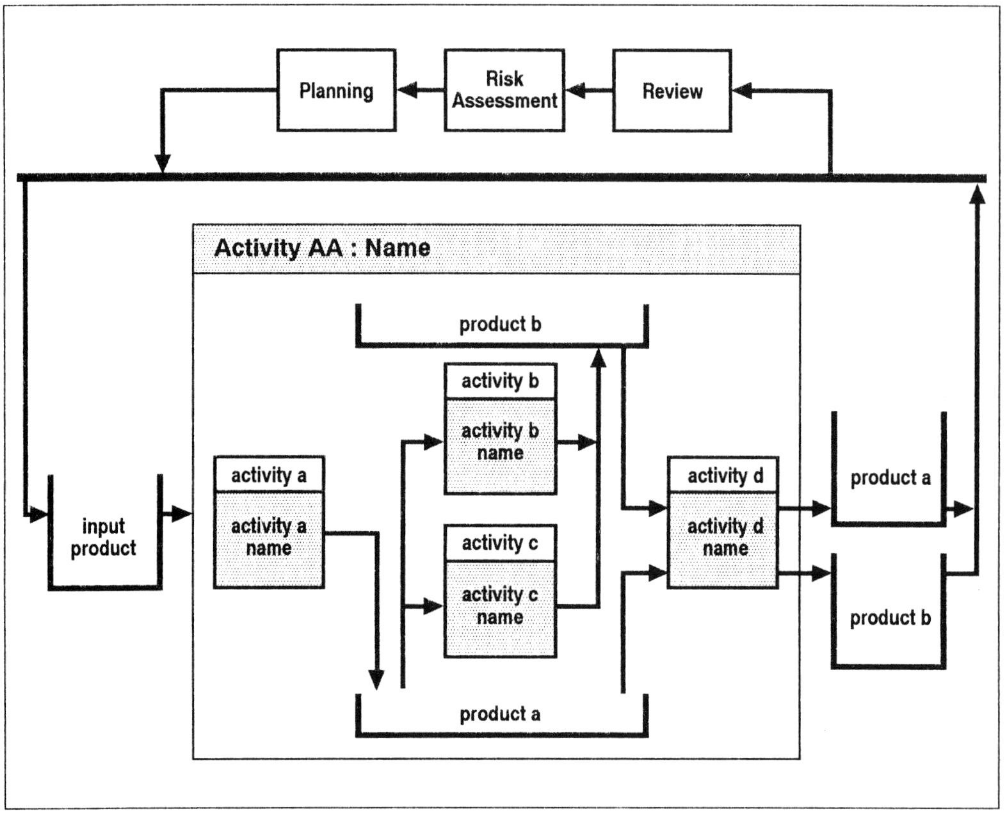

Figure 7.4: GEMINI work structure notation

Activities	An activity is represented as a rectangle with an associated identifier and activity name. The inputs needed to perform an activity enter the box representing the activity from the left and the outputs from the activity exit the box to the right. In the diagram, activity AA represents a major activity taking place within the development sector of the spiral model. The review, risk assessment and planning sectors are shown above the line, representing the complete set of activities associated with the spiral model. The figure illustrates that these are repeating activities where the same tasks take place each time, albeit in respect of a different set of products and development activities. Each of the activities in the development sector may also be the subject of a spiral. The output products from major activities pass into the review sector activities.
Products	An intermediate or project product is illustrated as an open tray with the name of the product.
Flows of products and/or information	Activities generate products and require certain inputs to be provided, either products from other activities or external documents. This flow is represented as a set of arrowed lines between activities and products.

In some cases, a diagram would become incomprehensible if all the product flows were drawn directly. Labels have been introduced to overcome this. Pictorially, these are identifiers enclosed in circles. The identifier in the circle is that of the activity to which the arrowed line would be drawn. Figure 7.5 shows an example of this.

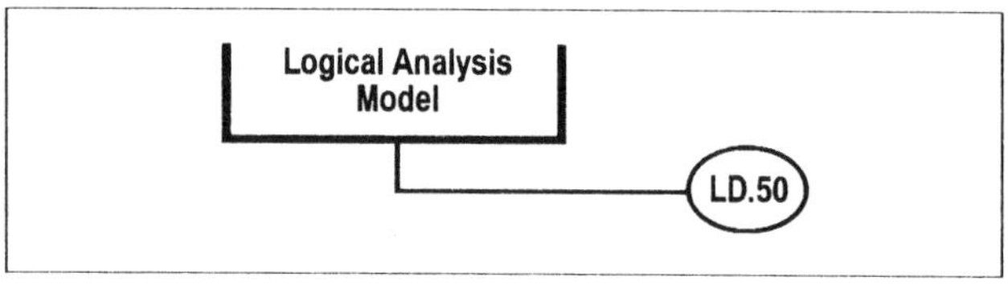

is equivalent to:

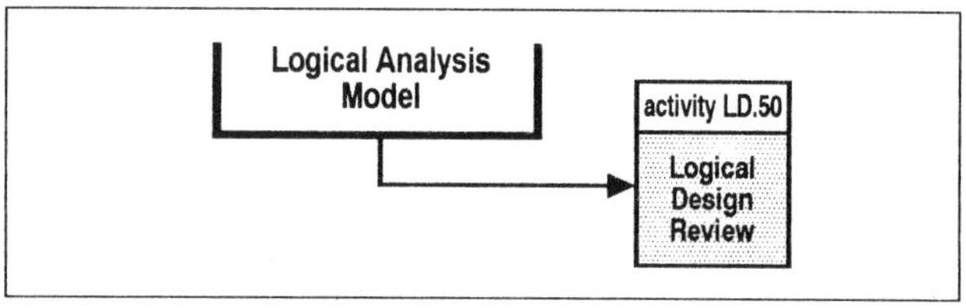

Figure 7.5: Work structure flow notation

The *GEMINI Technical Reference* volume contains fuller descriptions of the products to be developed in a GEMINI project, and the work structures for the activities which develop them.

7.5 Use of plans

The overall Project Plan is the responsibility of the Project Controller and is approved by the Project Board. It provides a communication vehicle between the Project Board, the Project Controller and the Project Manager. To facilitate control, the Project Manager provides information on actual resource usage and progress which are monitored by the Project Controller against the estimates. The plan is annotated with actual resource usage as a project proceeds. Comparison of actual resource usage against plans should be used to refine plans for future work on the project, and to help improve project planning for future projects.

The Project Controller assesses the appropriateness of the activities to be used by the supply side to develop products to be passed to the demand side. The Project Manager supplies information to facilitate this process and agrees products to be delivered; in terms of content, coverage, structure and format.

Proper planning ensures that the required resources are available at the appropriate time.

Any unplanned situations must be highlighted by flagging them and documenting a Project Issue Report. Issues must be referred to the Project Controller for assessment, and an Exception Plan may have to be drawn up.

Exception Plans are produced and used in a GEMINI project in the same way as they are produced and used in standard PRINCE. The Exception Plan relates to a GEMINI spiral circuit in the way that it would relate to a PRINCE stage.

Plans are updated to reflect any actions approved for addressing the issues raised.

Progress Reports must be produced by the Project Manager to reflect what has actually been achieved. These reports are used to monitor the actual resource usage and as a basis for planning activities for future work.

Plans in the CID, and Development Sector Plans for the project-level spiral, are used in a similar way to the overall Project Plan.

Lower-level plans may be internal to the supply side under the Project Manager's control. These should be used in a similar way to the plans under the Project Controller's control.

7.6 Summary

Project planning documents should be clear and succinct; they should concentrate on the products to be delivered. When a Project Plan is evaluated, it should be clear that:

- they define the products that meet the requirements of this project
- they define the activities that will lead to those products
- they include realistic estimates of the resources needed for those activities.

Planning is essential to the success of any project. The Project Controller has responsibility for project-level planning with input from the Project Manager. The Project Manager must ensure that the Development Team work to the agreed plans and carry out the detailed planning, within supply side responsibility.

8 Production management

8.1 Introduction

This chapter describes issues relating to the activities which are to be carried out within the development sector of the project management process model. These activities must be managed and controlled to ensure that the correct items are produced and resources are used effectively.

Appropriate techniques are specific to the needs of a project. This chapter gives guidance on issues which need to be considered when choosing the techniques to use on a particular project.

8.1.1 Production management

Production management is the administration of all the resources needed to develop the Technical Products which are required to fulfil the objectives of the project.

What to produce

A KBS development project can be defined in terms of a set of products which need to be produced. This set includes Technical Products which are used in the analysis and design of the application. There are eight models which are major Technical Products to be produced. These models are briefly described in section 8.3, with fuller descriptions in the volume *GEMINI Technical Reference.*

How to develop

Having defined the Technical Products which are to be developed the techniques to develop them must be chosen.

The Technical Products are primarily concerned with transforming knowledge from requirement to solution.

An approach to KBS development which relied upon transforming application specific knowledge directly into implementation specific representations would be very tedious indeed, since each transformation would be unique to that application. In addition, the implementation specific representation would bias the analysis and interpretation of the knowledge. The application specific knowledge would be made to fit the implementation specific representation.

GEMINI guidance is intended to be used for projects in a wide range of application areas, with each implemented using the most appropriate technology.

Products of the early parts of a project need to be represented in a way which is largely dependent on the characteristics of the type of application (application specific). Products in the latter parts of a project need to be represented in a way conducive to the technology to be used for implementation (implementation specific).

Thus, in GEMINI, inferences are first identified as being representative of a specific type of knowledge and then abstracted to a form and structure which is quite independent of their origin. Once this analysis is complete, the choice of representation for the implementation environment, for example rules and frames, can be made based on the requirements of the application rather than on the way in which the application requirements are expressed.

GEMINI development models represent different stages in the translation process. The products of the early part of the project may be highly application specific in the way they are represented. Products during the latter stages tend to be dependent on the technology used to implement the final system.

How to deliver

Several of the Technical Products will be delivered by the supply side to the demand side during the course of the project. The content, structure and format of these deliverables must be formally agreed between the two parties. The demand side need to be able to establish the acceptability of deliverables. Test requirements may affect the choice of Technical Products and the techniques appropriate to their development.

The Project Manager must ensure that all products are developed according to their product description. Deliverables must be passed to the demand side in a form that makes this conformance demonstrable.

8.1.2 The importance of production management decisions

The demand side specifies the project requirements in terms of the products which must be delivered by the supply side. The choice of techniques is an issue for the Project Manager to resolve. The supply side must be able to demonstrate that they can produce the deliverables to the standard required by the Project Controller within timetable and budget.

The supply side must undertake appropriate testing of the deliverables before delivery. The demand side will also need to undertake testing activities as part of their review process. The Project Manager needs to be aware of the implications of demand side testing on the products to be delivered. Their format requirements may be affected or may affect the tests.

System maintenance

The demand side is concerned with maintenance of the implemented KBS. The supply side should ensure that the Project Controller is made aware of any system maintenance implications during design and documentation of project products. System maintenance covers all activities concerned with making any future change to an existing computer system.

The analysis and design products provide information which can be used for maintenance activities. How maintenance is to be carried out and who is to undertake it may influence the requirements for the analysis and design products.

8.2 Technical Products

Technical Products are used to capture information about the application during the course of the project. GEMINI defines a set of Technical Products which capture the required details. In a particular project, the contents of an individual product may vary from the contents defined in GEMINI. It is important to make sure that the required information for the whole project is included within the complete set of identified products.

The Project Manager is responsible for development of those Technical Products that document analysis and design. These are the Application Products. Other Technical Products may be developed by the supply side or by the demand side with the Project Manager's assistance.

The Project Manager agrees the products to be delivered with the Project Controller, together with format and timescales. This set of deliverables may not include all of the Technical Products developed by the supply side, as some of the Technical Products are intermediate products used to produce deliverables. The demand side will need deliverables to provide all the information required to maintain the KBS.

Products may go through several versions before they are regarded as stable, for delivery to the demand side. It is therefore important to ensure that a suitable approach to version control is adopted by the Development Team.

8.2.1 Technical Products Breakdown

The top level of the *Technical Products Breakdown* contains the major products of the development process (See Figure 8.1).

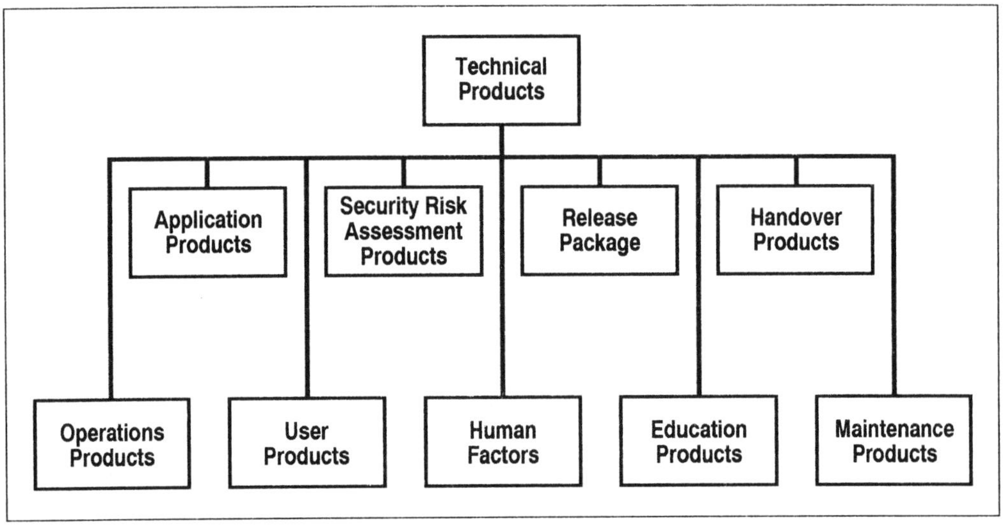

Figure 8.1 Technical Products Breakdown Structure

Some Technical Products do not contribute directly to the developed KBS. These are products which are required to support development of an effective working final system. For example, Education Products are developed to ensure that everyone connected with the system receives appropriate training. Training is a necessary project activity which must be scheduled and resourced to achieve the project objectives.

The supply side may provide details for inclusion in any of these products, but will generally concentrate on the development of Application Products. The supply side responsibilities for developing or contributing to products must be defined and agreed from the outset of the project.

8.2.2 Operations Products

Operations Products define the environment within which the applications are to run. These may be produced externally to the project or may already be in place. Nevertheless, they are documented and subject to the same change control and configuration management procedures as other products in the project.

Products in this category include:

- capacity planning products
- hardware environment
- operating guide
- communications environment
- take-on data
- operating software
- application software
- operator training
- service-level agreements.

8.2.3 Application Products

Application Products are those normally associated with the development of the system. These include analysis, design and implementation products (see section 8.3).

8.2.4 User Products

User Products provide the information that a user needs to be able to use the system. The User Guide explains how the system can be used and may act as both a training document and a reference manual. Information on issues such as siting of equipment may also be relevant here.

8.2.5 Security Risk Assessment Products

The *Security Risk Assessment Products* should be developed using a risk analysis method such as CCTA's CRAMM.

Steps can be taken to ensure that assets controlled by the system are safeguarded, by examining possible security risks and deciding what to do about them. The risks and counter-measures must be addressed within the requirements for the final system, so they need to be documented clearly and appropriately for future access.

8.2.6 Human Factors

The *Human Factors* products are used to prescribe ergonomic and job specification factors which need to be considered when designing the system.

These products should cover any aspect of the system which has an impact on people. Ideally, there will be overall standards set within an organisation to cover areas like ergonomics, job design and the human/computer interface. These standards need to be applied to each project and, where necessary, tailored to ensure that the specific user requirements can be met.

8.2.7 Education Products

Education Products are those necessary to teach the appropriate people how to work with the system. All the people concerned with the system must be considered for training.

8.2.8 Handover Products

Handover Products are those products which need to be passed on at the end of the project so that the system can continue to run and undergo change. The Handover Products include documentation about the system design and implementation as well as the Operations, User and Education Products already mentioned.

8.2.9 Release Package

The *Release Package* is the set of products which must be given to the operations staff so that a running system can be installed.

8.2.10 Maintenance Products

The *Maintenance Products* consist of documents to support maintenance of the operational system. Maintenance of knowledge is a particular issue for KBS. Documentation needs to be provided to define who is responsible for identifying possible changes, where the new knowledge comes from and how control is exercised to prevent out-of-date knowledge being used.

8.3 Application Products Breakdown

Application Products are those Technical Products that result from the activities to develop the system (see Figure 8.2).

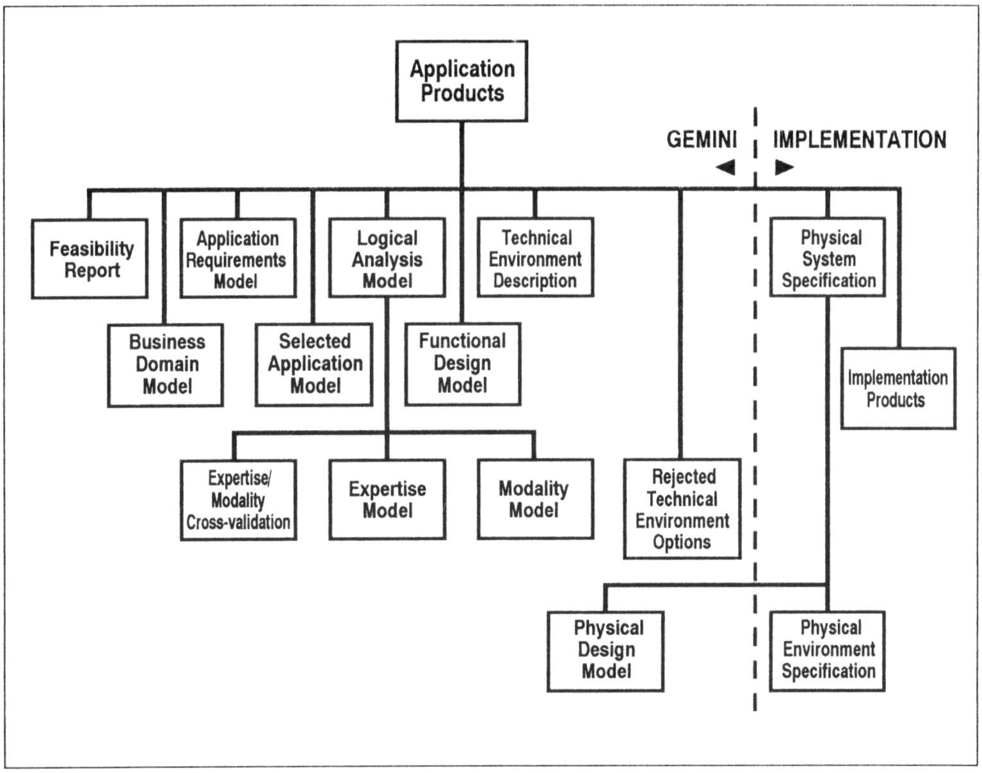

Figure 8.2: Application Products Breakdown Structure

These products include:

- the project documentation of the analysis and design activities, in this case GEMINI products
- the working physical system with its associated documentation.

A system is built by developing several products as shown in Figure 8.2. Each of these products concentrates on a particular area of information.

Brief descriptions of the GEMINI products shown in Figure 8.2 are given in the following subsections. Additional detail is given in the *GEMINI Technical Reference* volume.

8.3.1 Feasibility Report

The *Feasibility Report* records whether or not the users' needs can be reasonably met by the proposed system. There are three aspects to feasibility:

- business
- organisational
- technical.

8.3.2 Business Domain Model

The *Business Domain Model* is a representation of the organisational structure and business functions. The scope of possible applications may be identified based on this representation. The impact of a potential system on the organisation can be clarified and the resulting revised Business Domain Model defined. The Business Domain Model covers both current and proposed systems and requirements.

This product brings all the various requirements lists together into one place. Its purpose is to allow an overview of all requirements, making conflicts and redundancies more visible 'at a glance'.

8.3.3 Application Requirements Model

The *Application Requirements Model* holds a specification of the required external behaviour of the system, together with the organisational, operational, technical and resource constraints which affect the way that the system is to be designed and implemented.

The requirements will reflect the overall nature of the application. Generally, conventional requirements analysis techniques will provide the necessary level of information.

8.3.4 Selected Application Model

The *Selected Application Model* is a representation of the tasks and data flows in an application. This representation provides a more precise definition of the functionality of the proposed application than the Business Domain Model.

The Selected Application Model is a scoping document, which concerns itself with the size, complexity, difficulty and tractability of a specific application. It represents the first detailed look at technical feasibility, and establishes costs for the development of an application. This product will identify which elements of the application are suitable for KBS development.

For one application, this product consists of description, scope, objectives, constraints, jobs and tasks of that application.

8.3.5 Expertise Model

The *Expertise Model* holds a description of the knowledge (expertise) to be encoded into the implemented KBS.

It draws together information which the Expert feels is appropriate for this application. It specifies the processing requirements in terms of strategic, tactical and inference information and defines the data components.

8.3.6 Modality Model

The *Modality Model* defines interactions in the proposed system. *Agents* are persons or other systems that interact with or are components of the proposed system. The Modality Model defines agents, details which tasks each performs and indicates how the agents interact. It models when the agents can ask for or give information. The pattern of interaction between agents is known as modality.

This product is used to ensure that user requirements and technical interface possibilities are evaluated at the same time and tasks are allocated effectively.

The product is important in managing the users' expectations of the system and providing a guide to user interface design.

8.3.7 Logical Analysis Model

The *Logical Analysis Model* is the pivotal product in a GEMINI-based project. It brings together the Expertise Model and the Modality Model into a single validated whole. The expert and user views of the application are drawn together and cross-validated to ensure that a coherent specification is built for the application. In addition to the Expertise Model and the Modality Model, the Logical Analysis Model contains the documentation of the Expertise/Modality Cross-validation.

The Logical Analysis Model forms the basis for the further design of the KBS. It is constructed before physical design constraints are considered which means that within this model the application knowledge is defined in terms which are independent of the implementation environment.

8.3.8 Functional Design Model

The *Functional Design Model* is a revision of the Logical Analysis Model. The revision reflects design decisions concerning how individual components of the system will be implemented. For example, a rule-based approach may result in a very different functional design from an object-oriented approach.

The Functional Design Model is independent of any particular implementation environment. The model does not pre-empt the choice of features to be available in the hardware and software used for development and implementation of the operational KBS.

8.3.9 Technical Environment Description

The *Technical Environment Description* (TED) contains a definition of the requirements of the environment in which the application is to be developed and will run. The TED supports the Application Requirements Model by providing information on how the application requirements can be met. The information includes a description of the features that the hardware and software must support (for example, if the user interface is to be based on windows).

The features described include KBS and non-KBS elements. There must be information on system sizing, performance, data security and recovery, as the TED must provide sufficient information to support equipment procurement.

8.3.10 Rejected Technical Environment Options

The *Rejected Technical Environment Options* provide management with a record of the options for the implementation of the system which were analysed but not recommended. This supports the choice of the particular approach to implementation being advocated. This information can be used during the selection of the actual hardware and system software.

8.3.11 Physical Design Model

The *Physical Design Model* provides a representation of all the components and functions of the system to be implemented. It is implementation dependent, the design details being dependent on the technical environment chosen for implementation.

Much of this detail is portrayed diagrammatically using, for example, state transition diagrams. Approaches to user interface design may include (controlled) prototyping.

8.3.12 Physical Environment Specification

The *Physical Environment Specification* is a detailed description of the implementation environment. The information for this product is usually provided by the vendor.

8.3.13 Physical System Specification

The *Physical System Specification* comprises the Physical Design Model (which is produced within GEMINI (see section 8.3.11), and the Physical Environment Specification, which is not.

8.3.14 Implementation Products

Implementation Products provide the detail necessary to set up the final working system, so that it adheres to the user requirements. Much of the detail here is augmented by the Operations Products, User Products and Handover Products (see section 8.2).

8.4 Development of Technical Products

The Project Manager is responsible for providing the demand side with the identified products. These products are defined by the Project Controller, in terms of format, structure and content. The details must be agreed with the Project Controller before development starts.

There is no prescriptive set of correct techniques for use within GEMINI. Choice of techniques must be based on their applicability to the project. The Project Manager is likely to be advising the Project Controller on the suitability of techniques to be used in development.

8.4.1 Techniques

Chapter 8 of the volume *GEMINI Technical Reference* discusses available techniques. That chapter provides guidance on techniques available for KBS development and shows where they can be used, focusing on KBS specific techniques. Some of these techniques are expansions or extensions of techniques used in conventional analysis and design. The rest of section 8.4 gives some indication of the way KBS specific techniques are covered in that chapter.

Techniques are considered in three areas familiar to KBS project teams:

- knowledge acquisition
- knowledge representation
- KBS validation.

A wide variety of techniques in each of these areas are detailed, followed by general guidance on the selection of techniques and discussion of key factors in their selection for the main GEMINI models.

8.4.2 Knowledge acquisition techniques

Knowledge acquisition is the term commonly applied to the process by which KBS Development Teams gain an understanding of the expertise in the business area of concern.

The number and variety of sources of knowledge required to develop the system must be identified and the knowledge acquired in three main ways:

- elicitation from Experts
- extraction from documents
- derivation from data.

Techniques are detailed for each of these, in respect of sources of knowledge, in Chapter 8 of the volume *GEMINI Technical Reference.*

8.4.3 Knowledge representation techniques

Knowledge representation refers to the formalisms that are adopted to record expertise in a structured form. This abstraction of the knowledge forms the basis for its incorporation in KBS. Significantly, the largest proportion of KBS to date have been built using a combination of just three knowledge representation techniques:

- Production Rules
- Frames
- First Order Predicate Logic.

These techniques are described, together with other less established techniques, in Chapter 8 of the volume *GEMINI Technical Reference.*

8.4.4 KBS validation techniques

It is a common fallacy that validation can only take place after a system has been developed. For KBS, even more than for conventional systems, there is a continual need to evaluate the analysis and design decisions against the requirements.

KBS present some particularly challenging validation problems. KBS projects also make use of the full range of conventional testing techniques, for example inspection, unit testing, integrated testing and regression testing.

A particular problem with knowledge based systems is the issue of reconciling any differences:

- within a group of experts
- within a group of users
- between users and experts.

The views of differing experts need to be merged when more than one expert is involved. The same knowledge acquisition techniques must be used with each expert and the same knowledge representation techniques used to document the results. Any differences have to be identified and analysed as they may represent important knowledge. The knowledge incorporated into the KBS must be an agreed consolidation of all expert views.

Users may have different requirements as well as different levels of experience in the domain and application that the KBS is to address. All the relevant views need to be represented so that each user can operate the system in an appropriate way.

Experts, even if they are potential users of the developed system, are likely to have a specific view of a KBS, which may be very different from the views of non-expert users. The views of experts and users must be reconciled. By using agreed standards for documenting knowledge, this reconciliation is made more feasible. This improves the ultimate quality of the system by ensuring the user requirements are consistent with the expert views of the underlying knowledge.

If differences cannot be satisfactorily resolved by the User, Expert and Knowledge Engineers, then demand side management may need to adjudicate.

8.4.5 Assessing techniques

Project Controllers are unlikely to be proficient in techniques specific to KBS development and may rely on the Project Manager to provide information to assess the appropriateness of various techniques for each product.

Once the techniques have been chosen, the activities required to produce each product can be specified to the appropriate level of detail.

Guiding principles

The Project Manager must assure Project Controller that:

- techniques have a specific purpose with a clearly defined objective, such as the enhancement of the detail of a particular product
- the same technique is used to describe the same type of information in different products. There should be no unnecessary transformations from one technique to another. There may be different representation techniques that show the same type of information from other perspectives; but the same technique should be used to show the same information from the same perspective

- the techniques used aid communication between the various participants in the project
- the techniques are established, mature and understood by the Knowledge Engineers
- the techniques used will facilitate maintenance of the KBS after implementation.

Some KBS Development Teams are accustomed to working with a restricted set of techniques and tools. The demand side may have a standard set of techniques and tools to be used for KBS development. This standardisation can reduce costs and improve the maintainability of applications by limiting the skill requirements. Organisations may still have to consider techniques outside this range when:

- application requirements demand solutions that go beyond the scope of their current standards
- new techniques become available which potentially fit within the standards.

The range of techniques that are approved by the organisation may be limited because many techniques are not widely used. This limitation may be due to their specialised nature, labour intensiveness, computational intensiveness, or lack of support by appropriate tools. The Project Manager may recommend a given technique for a variety of reasons, including:

- familiarity with the technique and recognising its fit with the planned development
- availability of tool support for the chosen technique, possibly reducing the cost of the project
- the requirements dictate the use of one specific technique

- the demand organisation's standardisation on particular techniques
- availability of specific skills.

All options should be considered fully and the basis of the recommendation recorded. Once techniques have been chosen for developing products, the required activities to develop these products can be defined.

Significance of knowledge representation decision

The choice of *knowledge representation technique* is often one of the most significant decisions in the project as it can constrain the physical implementation. It can also influence the form of the knowledge acquisition techniques. A good choice of representation technique will enable the rapid definition of all necessary knowledge and its transformation into effective software. A bad choice may require a wasteful translation process or make unrealistic performance demands on hardware. Some KBS exist that exploit the strengths of more than one knowledge representation formalism to good effect.

8.5 Testing

The Project Controller is responsible for acceptance testing of the system and for dealing with any implications this has for system handover. The Project Manager is responsible for ensuring that the required features can be demonstrated to the demand side. Supply side resources will be required for the acceptance testing and any necessary reworking.

The demand side is responsible for specification of the tests to be conducted. A standard set of test cases is likely to be required, and should be provided by the Domain Team. The Project Manager may find it useful for experts to provide some test data for supply side testing, prior to release of products.

These issues are a major concern of project quality management (see Chapter 5).

8.6 Summary

The Project Manager is responsible for the development of the products required by the Project Controller.

Techniques provide repeatable means of producing products. Appropriate techniques are specific to the needs of a project. The issues highlighted in this chapter should be considered when choosing the techniques to use on a particular project.

At project initiation the major products for the project are identified. These are the Technical Products which must be developed by the supply side during the project. There will be implications for system testing and long term maintenance which must be considered when identifying the content, structure and format of the required deliverables.

Approaches to developing the deliverables will be finalised, during initial negotiations between the supply and demand sides, prior to project planning.

9 Project integration

9.1 Introduction

This chapter discusses the issues involved in integrating development of KBS with development of conventional IT systems. It does not explicitly cover the technical issues associated with the development of KBS systems to interface with existing applications or infrastructure facilities such as DBMS, TPMS and user interface products. Such interfacing requirements place constraints on options for the KBS project. Much of the information in this chapter can be useful in addressing the needs of such development projects.

The Project Manager must be able to control all streams of work associated with a KBS development, including the merging of streams during the latter stages of the project.

9.1.1 Project integration

Project integration refers to the development of an implementable system which combines KBS and conventional IT approaches. Integration may involve techniques for the analysis and design or techniques and tools for implementation.

The developed KBS and conventional IT components must work together to solve a business problem. Working together may involve the sharing of data or the co-operation of processes.

The requirement for the components to work together means that a number of technical issues need to be addressed by the project:

- how the KBS design fits with the conventional IT design
- how information will be passed between the components, for example, through access to a database or by parameters

- whether the techniques for implementing the KBS can work with the techniques for implementing the conventional IT system
- whether a tried and tested interface exists between the KBS environment and the conventional IT environment.

Techniques for analysis and design and techniques and tools for implementation should be chosen to enable a simple interaction between the two components.

There are two other important issues:

- co-ordinating two different approaches, especially during analysis and design
- ensuring the end products are complete and consistent.

A Project Manager will, generally, have the main responsibility for decisions about the techniques used to develop particular products. However, sometimes the supply organisation may be involved in only a small part of the overall project and so have to abide by decisions taken by the demand side for the project as a whole.

9.1.2 When to address project integration

Project integration must be considered throughout a development project, particularly in assessing:

- the *feasibility* of solving business problems using IT
- how the *analysis* activities can be accomplished
- the representations to be used for system *design*, in particular system interfaces
- *testing* of separate components and the integrated system
- *implementation* particularly where new technology is being introduced into an existing operating (business) environment.

The last two are outside the scope of GEMINI but the Project Manager needs to be aware that these issues will be of importance to the demand side.

9.2 Integration perspectives

In any IS development project the primary objective is to achieve full integration of all the elements of the system at system level. In a project with KBS and conventional IT elements, full integration at the system level will ensure that the KBS elements co-operate effectively with the conventional IT elements. The degree of mutual dependence determines the significance of integration as a project concern. The level of dependence of conventional components on KBS components may be:

- total dependence. The system will not operate effectively without a KBS component
- independent functionality. The system will provide useful functionality without a KBS component
- adjustable. Some of the functionality which was to have been provided by the KBS might be supplied in alternative ways.

KBS components may have similar levels of dependence on conventional components. The level of dependence correlates with the level of risk inherent in developing the system. The amount of co-ordination necessary to ensure the whole system is developed successfully is determined by the dependencies between the components.

9.2.1 Integration through underlying technology

Integration is a more critical consideration, the more closely coupled the system is to be when implemented. The main issues are:

- *logical dependencies*. There may be a number of logical dependencies between the KBS and other components
- *data dependencies*. The components of integrated systems typically need to have access to common data
- *timing dependencies*. There may be a need to co-ordinate the performance of the components to ensure that outputs are provided in a timely way.

These dependencies will have implications for design. There are also issues which may constrain the technical choices available:

- *technical constraints*. The techniques and tools with which the major components are being developed and the policies and standards being used may impose constraints on the development options for the others
- *the presence of existing systems*. A project may involve the addition of knowledge based system functionality to an existing system, constraining the operational environment and the interfacing options
- *staff attachment to conventional technology*. Problems in the implemented system are likely to be blamed on the more novel technology of KBS.

The techniques used and the way they are applied can help to address integration issues:

- *global data models* may be available with data modelling elements suitable for the KBS and conventional IT components
- *extended data flow* diagrams may be able to define the relationships between KBS and conventional IT components
- *interfacing standards* may be available to define the flow of data and control between the components
- *performance standards* may be used to ensure that any timing dependencies are met.

If it is possible to use the same types of tool for the implementation of both types of components, many of the technical issues will be resolved. Management of the two streams should take advantage of any possibilities in this area at the time of selection of the technical environment.

9.2.2 Documentation techniques

There must be a good level of communication between the two streams of work. There are two views of a system which are critical:

- the data view
- the process view.

In a joint project, it is important that the techniques used to represent these elements of the KBS are compatible with those of conventional software engineering. In many cases this can be achieved through the use of techniques which are expansions of conventional software engineering techniques, such as extended dataflow modelling and extended data modelling.

9.2.3 Technical standards

To ensure that the two system components are able to function together, it is important to define how to integrate the components technically. At an early stage in the project, this should be documented by detailing:

- technical standards for system interfaces
- performance and other non-functional standards for the combined system
- performance standards for the system elements providing response to each other.

The technical standards should specify how the two elements will communicate by identifying for each interaction :

- the element that triggers the interaction
- how information will be passed
- the normal sequence of communication
- abnormal communications such as error conditions
- how the interaction terminates.

9.3 Project control

Integrated systems are more complex to build than stand-alone KBSs. The Project Manager has a responsibility to identify and quantify the technical risks involved in undertaking a dual stream project. The non-KBS stream may well be managed by another Project Manager.

The Project Manager needs to consult with the Project Controller to ensure that both streams of work share a common set of objectives and are properly planned. The Project Plans must contain clear descriptions of:

- dependencies between system components and between project activities
- means of communication between the two streams, including common review and control points

- provisions for merging of the two streams of work
- adequate provision for integration and testing of system components.

The Project Manager proposes an approach for the KBS stream. Information on the techniques used or proposed in the non-KBS stream will be needed from the demand side as input to these proposals. If the documentation standards for data and process modelling are not compatible provision may be required to translate between the notations so that the KBS Development Team can understand the functionality of the overall system. Similarly the non-KBS development team will need information from the KBS development activities. It is the Project Controller's responsibility, with the Project Manager's support, to make decisions to ensure that the approaches are compatible.

Proper provision must be made for regular communication between the two project teams. Frequent communication is the most effective way of identifying issues at an early stage and ensuring that they are effectively resolved.

9.4 Summary

In a KBS development project, the Project Manager may be required to advise the Project Controller on all technical aspects of integrating the KBS with other systems.

Annexes

A The role of the Project Manager

A.1 Prime responsibility

The Project Manager is responsible for ensuring that the supply side delivers, to the Project Controller, the required products to the required standards of quality, within specified constraints of time and cost.

A.2 Main activities

Reporting to the Project Controller: to maintain demand side management awareness of project status, and in particular of any important issues which have arisen.

Assisting in the process of setting up an agreed interface with the demand side organisation.

Liaising closely with the Project Controller: to provide assurance that work is progressing to plan. This is achieved by presenting an assessment of the current situation and plans to resolve any issues arising.

Communicating the quality requirements of the project to the development team: to ensure adherence to the quality assurance statement contained in the Project Initiation Document

Maintaining supply side management awareness of project progress and issues: to ensure readiness to deal with issues, should any escalation up the organisation become necessary.

Monitoring and controlling resources to ensure that development activities stay within budget and timescales.

Ensuring that products conform to requirements before delivery to the demand side.

Project Manager tasks

Some of the tasks allocated to the Project Manager role in a standard PRINCE environment are undertaken in GEMINI by the Project Controller. The GEMINI Project Manager tasks include:

- liaising with the Project Controller to assure the overall direction and integrity of the project
- agreeing technical and quality approaches with the Project Controller
- assisting in definition and agreement of the supply/demand interface
- providing input for the Circuit Initiation Document, to the Project Controller
- agreeing project objectives for technical activities
- planning the development activities and agreeing the plans with the Project Controller
- defining objectives and responsibilities for each Team Leader
- delivering required products to quality criteria on time and to budget
- monitoring overall progress and initiating corrective action where necessary
- managing the use of those resources under supply side control
- advising the Project Controller of deviations from plan at all levels and proposing corrective action
- where corrective action cannot be completely accommodated within tolerances, submitting appropriate Exception Plans to the Project Controller
- presenting regular Highlight Reports, Checkpoint Reports and Progress Reports to the Project Controller.

A.3 Control

The Project Manager is controlled by the Project Controller.

The Project Manager controls the Team Leaders.

A.4 Required knowledge and experience

To carry out the responsibilities listed the Project Manager needs to have project management skills and technical KBS skills.

The individual needs specific skills as follows:

- appropriate level of management experience
- project management experience
- good working knowledge of PRINCE
- understanding of demand side technical and quality standards
- familiarity with supply side technical and quality standards
- understanding of demand side IS strategy
- knowledge of a range of KBS techniques
- practical experience of KBS development.

The Project Manager needs to have practical experience of managing some KBS development activities. This will have been as a Team Leader or Project Manager. Some previous experience of deploying the GEMINI guidance would be useful.

B Project activities of a Project Manager

B.1 Introduction

The objectives of this annex are to explain what is required of a Project Manager with responsibility for a GEMINI based project.

Within a KBS project KBS development skills may be provided by an external supplier or a part of the business organisation separate from the demand side. The principles, for the supply side, are the same in each case, to ensure that the demand side users get what they need.

Within a KBS development project the supply side activities may be carried out, by one organisation, several different ones in parallel or different ones sequentially.

From the supply side viewpoint there are three distinct phases of a project. Each phase has its own management demands:

- start of supply side involvement (section B.2)
- development by the supply side (section B.3)
- end of supply side involvement (section B.4).

The Project Manager has specific responsibilities depending on the phase the project is in.

B.2 Start of supply side involvement

The start of supply side involvement in a project may coincide with project initiation or occur subsequently. The responsibilities of both supply and demand sides within the project must be agreed before the supply side starts development work.

The Project Manager takes part in, or advises on, any negotiations with the demand side. Agreement on the work required will be necessary whether the Development Team is part of the user organisation or external to it. An important part of this agreement will concern the demand/supply relationship and the Project Manager's part in this. The Project Manager's part may vary according to the technical knowledge available to the supply side. When the Development Team is supplied by a non-government organisation any agreements will form part of a formal contract.

B.2.1 Demand/supply negotiations

Details of what is to be produced, when and to what standard must be agreed and documented.

The Project Manager is responsible for the supply side's relationship with the Project Controller. The definition of this relationship is documented as part of an agreement, covering:

- the project organisation structure
- project plans and monitoring mechanisms
- control mechanisms
- requirements for delivery of the project products
- obligations and responsibilities.

When the relationship is governed by contract, this information forms part of the contractual documentation.

Much of this information is also contained in the Project Initiation Document (PID) described in B.2.2. Depending on when the project starts in relation to supply side involvement, the PID may form the basis for the supply/demand agreement.

B.2.2 Project Initiation Document

This documentation may have been produced prior to the Project Manager's assignment or during the early stages of the supply side involvement. In either case the Project Manager will have to be familiar with some of the contents of this document, which forms the basis of the project.

At the beginning of a project, the Project Controller ensures that several pieces of information are prepared and drawn together into a Project Initiation Document (PID) that is subject to Project Board approval. These pieces of information are:

- aims and objectives of the project
- project boundary
- project definition or functional definition
- quality assurance statement
- project organisation
- project plans.

The PID sets the overall ethos for the whole project. Annex C gives more details of its contents. The Project Manager will provide input to the PID, if the supply side is involved at project initiation. In any case the PID will provide input to the supply side Terms of Reference for the project.

Aims and objectives

This information relates the *project objectives* to the *business objectives* of the demand side and any threats or opportunities that it faces. The information includes a description of the *business benefits* expected in terms of quantifiable and unquantifiable benefits, together with the risks and costs. Any supply side activities must contribute to realising these benefits.

Project boundary	The project boundary details the scope of the project, its context and the constraints upon it including any relationships with other projects or systems. The supply side needs to be aware of the detail of any interfaces with other projects and take account of any interactions with other systems. Other constraints may include installation standards, current IT environment, availability of skills, government procedures, legislation and other external constraints.
Project definition	A project definition is an initial high-level description of the functional requirements of the system, qualified by non-functional requirements.
Quality assurance statement	The quality assurance statement (QAS) documents the overall approach to be taken by the Development Team to ensure that delivered products meet requirements, in terms of fitness for purpose and resourcing. The QAS specifies the quality requirements for the development and identifies the standards that must be met by the development team to ensure that the delivered products are acceptable. It specifies the quality requirements for the development. The supply side, through the Project Manager, may propose changes to the QAS, but these must be agreed by the Project Controller and approved by the Project Board. When the supply side has its own quality assurance regime, this will have to be fitted to demand side requirements and agreed by the Project Controller. There will be a list of major products and some specific, measurable targets for the project. The success criteria and deliverables of the project have to be agreed. These must be quantified in order to determine whether the objectives have been achieved.

Project organisation

The project organisation structure, responsibilities and lines of reporting must be agreed before work starts.

The Project Manager must propose suitable individuals to the demand side and provide relevant information on them. The demand side is responsible for ensuring that the project team is correctly constituted from the outset so that it will be able to resolve any problems encountered during system development. Part of this responsibility is to ensure that the individuals put forward from the supply side have appropriate skills and experience to carry out the required development activities.

The Project Manager must ensure that:

- every role within the supply side has been assigned to a competent individual who has the relevant skills and knowledge
- each team member is motivated to help the project succeed
- the team members are aware of their own and others' roles and responsibilities
- effective communication channels have been created within the project.

The Project Manager may be required to provide guidance on making any available choices of candidates for Domain Team roles.

The roles of User and Expert are particularly sensitive as either group may feel their job security threatened by the proposed KBS.

B.2.3 Project Plan

The high-level plan for a project is the pattern of activities and interactions to be used to achieve the project objectives, including the following:

- technical plans
- resource plans
- quality plans.

Further information on the contents of a plan are given in the product description in Annex C.

As part of the technical plans, there will be a list of major products to be developed during the project and an outline product description for each.

Product descriptions

Product descriptions are definitions of the Technical Products which are to be developed during the project. At project initiation, the product descriptions of products to be developed early in the project may be fairly detailed but the product descriptions of later products will not.

Before any agreement with the demand side is finalised the Project Manager must be clear on what products are required and be satisfied that the Development Team can produce them as specified. Some product descriptions, particularly relevant to the Project Manager, are given in Annex C. Further information concerning product descriptions is given in the volume *GEMINI Technical Reference*.

B.3 Development by the supply side

The Project Manager's main responsibility is to deliver products to the demand side which meet requirements within agreed budgets and timescales.

During development the Project Manager must monitor progress of development and communicate that progress to the Project Controller. The emphasis is to ensure that the work is carried out in accordance with the plans and the project management spiral model so that project activities follow the cycle of risk assessment, planning, development and review. This process enables monitoring of the development activities to take place, so that progress against plans and tolerances can be assessed.

The Project Manager must ensure the effectiveness of quality activities on the project. The Project Manager must also carry out regular checks to ensure that those activities are operating efficiently and effectively.

When new staff are brought into the Development Team the Project Manager must ensure that they satisfy the criteria laid down for the project and are satisfactory to the demand side.

The following mechanisms will be used to help with reviews of the status of the project:

- delivery details as agreed at the outset
- checkpoints
- exception reporting.

The Project Manager should ensure that this information is maintained and, where appropriate, passed on to the Project Controller.

B.3.1 Delivery details

Delivery details provide a record of every Technical Product with planned completion date, review date and acceptance date. Progress against these delivery details must be monitored, ready for the quality review and management sign-off. When appropriate, these products will then be delivered to the demand side for their review and acceptance, together with progress reports and information on resources used and activities carried out, which are then used to update the plans.

The change and version history of the products should also be stored, giving a complete change and version control for all the products of the project.

B.3.2 Checkpoints

Checkpoints are regular technical and management control points specified in the Project Plan. These can take the form of a paper report, or a meeting where minutes are produced.

Checkpoints cover information on budget status and exceptions to plan, such as late or early activity start and finish, and problems encountered.

The Project Controller will set major checkpoints with the Project Manager. Additionally the Project Manager will define checkpoints with the Development Team so that their output can feed into progress reports. Each delivery date will coincide with a major checkpoint.

B.3.3 Exception reporting

Mechanisms to capture details of unexpected situations during the development will be specified by the Project Controller and followed by the Project Manager. The Project Manager may also highlight exceptions which are not identified by the demand side specifications. This information is used to update the Project Plan on a regular basis. The Project Controller will require relevant information so that details can be given at Project Board meetings.

B.4 End of supply side involvement

The end of supply side involvement may coincide with project closure. The Project Manager may then be required to provide relevant information to the Project Controller for the project to be signed off and a project evaluation review to be carried out, following acceptance of all project deliverables by the demand side.

If the supply side is not involved in the full project, similar activities will take place covering the activities undertaken by the supply side.

B.4.1 Acceptance

The user organisation, through the demand side Project Board, will formally acknowledge the end of supply side involvement and acceptance of deliverables.

B.4.2 Project evaluation review

A review is carried out of the conduct of the project, highlighting problems and areas of success. This provides an assessment of the effectiveness of the management procedures used in the project. This assessment enables the experience gained and lessons learnt on the project to be applied to future projects.

For the supply side this may give information on how well the demand side thought they performed. There will be an evaluation of which aspects of the project could have been improved. For a commercial organisation this may help to focus the services that they provide to ensure more effective use of resources on future projects.

A *Post Implementation Review* (PIR) will take place some months after project closure but may not require supply side involvement.

B.4.3 Project Board acceptance of supply side work

A Project Board meeting takes place to coincide with or follow completion of work by the supply side. During this meeting, the objectives set out in the TOR are matched against what actually happened. The Project Board formally accepts the results and signs them off.

Before this meeting, the Project Manager must ensure that all deliverables are complete and have been accepted. The Project Controller produces a report for the Project Board giving the status of the project and the acceptability of the deliverables. The report contains a summary of the extent to which the objectives of the project have been met.

When the end of supply side involvement coincides with project closure, the last Project Board meeting of the project ends supply side involvement.

C Product descriptions

A set of products must be defined for each project. The documentation of the definitions is in the form of product descriptions. The product descriptions of particular relevance to the Project Manager are:

- Circuit Initiation Document
- Plan
- Project Initiation Document.

Guidance is given on the contents of these product descriptions in this annex.

C.1 Circuit Initiation Document (CID)

C.1.1 Purpose

The purpose of the Circuit Initiation Document is to gather together the information needed to control the work which is to be undertaken during a circuit of the spiral. This information includes defining the objectives and boundaries of the activities. The CID is the mechanism for conveying this information to the project team.

The information in the CID must be within the project boundary as set out in the PID and consistent with it. The latest CID forms the current project baseline and scopes the next circuit of the spiral. These details are an update of the previous baseline which was set in the PID or previous Circuit Initiation Documents. In this context, the CID is used during the next review phase to assess the progress which has been made in the current spiral circuit.

The CID for the following circuit of the spiral model is developed at the end of each review process. Management approval of this product is required before the next circuit of the spiral can commence.

C.1.2 Composition

In general, this document is a cut down version of the PID. The CID incorporates detailed information relevant to the next set of development activities as well as overall plans for the rest of the project.

Sections of the CID cover:

- aims and objectives
- project boundary
- functional definition
- quality assurance statement
- project organisation.

See the product description for a Product Initiation Document, for further details.

C.1.3 Derivation

The Circuit Initiation Document is derived from:

- the current Management Risk Assessment
- the Project Initiation Document
- the previous Circuit Initiation Document
- Progress Reports.

C.1.4 Quality

A CID is developed during each review sector for use in the next circuit of the spiral.

Criteria

The CID quality criteria include the following:

- is the composition as stated in the product description?
- are the names of personnel shown against the roles required?
- have the people named agreed to act and to commit the time as scheduled?
- have dates been set for all the control meetings and reports?
- have measures been proposed for all the risks identified for the project?
- have the Project Plans been reviewed and agreed?
- does the CID fit within the terms of reference as laid down in the Project Initiation Document?

Method

Formal review before submission to the relevant management level for approval.

C.1.5 External dependencies

Any external dependencies of the CID will be project specific.

C.2 Plan

C.2.1 Purpose

The purpose of a plan is to provide identification of the products which must be developed during the project or next development sector of the spiral model. There must be a specification of the activities needed to develop the identified products. A plan should provide a specification of how quality of the products will be assured as well as identifying the resources needed for quality control.

A plan shows the products, activities and resources required on a project or on an activity within a project. The plan forms an agreed baseline for the resource and scheduling requirements for the activities covered.

All plans are updated with actual resource usage as a project proceeds. The initial Project Plan forms a baseline which is the major reference for management to monitor the progress of activities throughout the project.

There are three types of plan:

- Project Plan
- Development Sector Plan
- Exception Plan.

The *Project Plan* sets out the overall approach which is to be taken on the project. The products and activities covered will be major ones.

A *Development Sector Plan* documents and schedules the resources required to develop the Technical Products covered by one circuit of the spiral.

An *Exception Plan* documents an unplanned situation that has arisen and records proposed corrective action.

C.2.2 Composition

Format and presentation will be in accordance with the organisation's or the site's standards. Plans will include some narrative of what is detailed and include an explanation of reasons for inclusion or exclusion of activities. Each plan should include technical, resource and quality aspects.

Technical plan

A technical plan shows the products to be developed and target completion dates given (elapsed timescales). Identified tolerances must be shown. Managers in charge of the development of the products will be identified. Dependencies between the project and other projects should be identified.

Technical plans may be documented by use of any of the following:

- Product Breakdown Structure supported by product descriptions
- Product Flow Diagram
- activity network or work structure supported by activity descriptions
- barchart
- graphical summary.

Resource plan

A resource plan shows estimates of amounts of each resource type required during each time period (predefined, may be monthly, weekly). These estimates should be based on the detail in the technical and quality plans.

Resource plans include the resourcing requirements for each activity and the whole project, including control tolerance details for the project.

Resource plans will include any of the following, as appropriate:

- table of resource requirements
- graphical summary
- cost tolerance recommendation
- project organisation details, that is roles and to whom they are assigned.

Quality plan

Quality plans include details of quality processes including product reviews, dates of checkpoint meetings and highlight report production. Names of reviewers should be identified, where possible.

Quality plans, developed in accordance with the quality assurance statement in the PID, include any of the following:

- timetable of major review points
- list of review participants and their role in the review
- formal or informal review using a review meeting or only written comments
- any additional information which needs to be taken into account by the review team. Note that quality review criteria should be included on the appropriate product description.

C.2.3 Derivation

The specific inputs depend upon the type of plan being developed. Typically, the inputs include:

- installation standards
- previous plans
- progress reports
- review assessments
- planning experience
- decisions based on Management Risk Assessment.

C.2.4 Quality

Criteria

The quality criteria for plans include:

- is the technical approach sound?
- is the plan feasible in terms of cost and time?
- is the plan up-to-date?
- does the technical plan match the resource plan?
- do both these plans match the quality plan?

Method

Formal quality review of the Project Plan before submission to the Project Board for approval.

Other plans to be reviewed before submission to the appropriate management level for approval.

C.2.5 External dependencies

The external dependencies of plans will largely be specific to the project circumstances and the level of the plan. They may include:

- planning expertise
- ability to identify skill requirements to carry through plan
- availability of information on skills available
- ability to schedule resources against competing commitments
- estimating expertise.

C.3 Project Initiation Document (PID)

C.3.1 Purpose

The purpose of the Project Initiation Document is to bring together the key information needed to start the project on a sound basis and to convey that information to all concerned with the project.

The Project Board must approve the Project Initiation Document (PID) before a project can formally start. The PID is a project management product designed to contain all the information required by a project team at the start of a new project.

The PID contains the project *terms of reference*. The PID contains the definition of the initial *project baseline* by detailing for project management the scope and objectives for the project along with a description of the overall approach to be taken.

C.3.2 Composition

The PID holds differing levels of detail depending on the type of project. For example, the PID for a Feasibility Study will be much less detailed than that for a Full Study.

Each PID is different but needs to include descriptions of the following:

- aims and objectives
- project boundary
- project definition or functional definition
- quality assurance statement
- project organisation.

The project plans cover the technical, resource and quality implications. These are appended to the PID and form an integral part of it.

Aims and objectives

This section provides details of the appropriate business objectives which the planned information system will support once it becomes operational. The information must include a description of the intended benefits, risks and costs of implementing the proposed information system. To provide a justification for the work, this section needs to include:

- *project objectives,* the goals that the project is intended to achieve. Critical requirements of the planned information system should be highlighted
- *business objectives,* the significant attainments that mark progress towards achieving the organisation's aims. The project management needs to be aware of relevant business objectives to ensure that the planned information system is consistent with them
- *business benefits,* the financial and non-financial benefits that are intended to accrue to the organisation through the implementation of the proposed information system. These benefits should be quantified to facilitate an objective assessment of the implemented system.

Project boundary

The project boundary provides a description of relationships with other projects and areas of common interest together with overviews of common outputs and inputs. This boundary includes the definition of possible constraints on the project, such as:

- installation standards recommending IT best practices for the organisation, for example:
  - national or departmental standards
  - installation practices

- existing IT environment. This includes details of hardware, and system and application software, currently used within the business area. Details may cover:
  - communication standards
  - data management
  - communication architecture
  - IT infrastructure
- information architecture. This aspect provides a description of a structure on which the information needs of the business can be implemented to make the best corporate use of information as a resource. Issues may include:
  - data dictionary standards to be used
  - the ownership of the data
  - data administration
  - Electronic Data Interchange
- plans for related products to provide information on issues of:
  - shared data
  - access requirements
  - capacity requirements
  - hardware availability
  - compatibility.

Project definition

The product definition or functional description is an initial outline description of the major deliverables of the project and the activities to develop them. The known requirements of the system are stated as the functional, or necessary operational features, which may be qualified by non-functional requirements.

This section is used to detail the methods and support techniques to be used for the analysis and design tasks.

Quality assurance statement

The quality assurance statement identifies the overall approach to be taken to ensure that the developed products are of an acceptable standard throughout the project.

There are four major aspects to the requirements to achieve prescribed quality. These are:

- identification of quality processes for the project, including references to applicable policies, codes of practice and standards
- determination of overall quality requirements for products and development activities, including formats, methods and applicable standards
- identification of the control mechanism to be used in the project to ensure the quality of products and control the use of resources. These control mechanisms include:
    - change control procedures
    - control points of Project Board interest including checkpoint meetings and highlight report production
    - tolerances
    - metrics
    - review procedures
- mechanisms for review and improvement of the quality processes for the project to ensure it fulfils its objectives.

These requirements cover issues such as how the Project Assurance Team will fulfil the role and how product reviews will be undertaken

Project organisation

The project organisation structure is defined in terms of roles. Where appropriate, individuals are assigned to these roles.

C.3.3 Derivation	The PID is derived from installation standards for project management taking account of GEMINI.
C.3.4 Quality	The PID is developed during the initial review of the project.
Criteria	The quality criteria for the PID include: • are all the components present? • are names shown against roles, where these can be identified at this stage of the project? • have the people named agreed to act and to commit the time as scheduled? • have dates been set for control meetings and report production? • have the Project Plans been quality reviewed and approved?
Method	Formal review before submission to Project Board for approval.
C.3.5 External dependencies	The external dependencies of a PID include: • existence of project management procedures • existence of installation standards.

Bibliography

CCTA Publications

PRINCE — *PRINCE Reference Manuals*, NCC Blackwell Ltd, (1990), ISBN: 1 85554 012 6

SSADM — *SSADM Version 4 Reference Manuals*, NCC Blackwell Ltd (1990), ISBN: 1 85554 004 5

CRAMM — An *Overview of CRAMM* (1992) is available from the CCTA Library.

Information Systems — The Information Systems Guides, published by John Wiley & Sons Ltd, Baffins Lane, Chichester PO19 1UD.

The following set of guides is referenced in this publication:

- *CCTA IS Guides Set B: Systems Development Set*, ISBN: 0 471 92556 X

Information Systems Engineering Library — The Information Systems Engineering Library provides guidance on managing and carrying out Information Systems Engineering activities. Relevant publications published by HMSO:

- *Improving the Maintainability of Software* (1993) ISBN: 0 11 330585 0

The foundation volumes of the GEMINI guidance consist of three volumes:

- *GEMINI: Controlling KBS Development Projects - Guidance for business-side project controllers*, ISBN: 0 11 330591 5
- *GEMINI: Managing KBS Development Projects - Guidance for IS-provider project managers*, ISBN: 0 11 330592 3
- *GEMINI Technical Reference - Guidance for KBS development project teams*, ISBN: 0 11 330593 1

Quality Management Library	The Quality Management Library (1992), published by HMSO as a five volume boxed set, ISBN: 0 11 330569 9
Appraisal and Evaluation Library	The Appraisal and Evaluation Library is a set of volumes which helps organisations to identify the products, particularly software, which best meet their requirements. Relevant volumes are: • *Overview and Procedures (1990),* ISBN 0 11 330534 6 • *Knowledge Based Systems (1990),* ISBN 0 11 330570 2
IT Infrastructure Library (ITIL)	ITIL is a series of books about how to provide quality IT services, and on the accommodation and environmental facilities needed to support IT. Relevant titles include: • *Capacity Management (1991),* ISBN: 0 11 330544 3 • *Configuration Management (1989),* ISBN: 0 11 330530 3 • *Change Management (1990),* ISBN: 0 11 330525 7 • *Testing an IT Service for Operational Use (1993),* ISBN: 0 11 330560 5

Other Publications

Boehm, BW, *A Spiral Model of Software Development and Enhancement*, Computer, May 1988

Ernst & Young US, *Ernst & Young Navigator System Series^{SM} Methodology Overview Monograph,* Ernst & Young, (1990)

Ernst & Young, *STAGES - Structured techniques for the analysis and generation of expert systems,* Ernst & Young (1991)

Hickman et al, *Analysis for knowledge-based systems: a practical guide to the KADS methodology,* Ellis Horwood, (1989)
ISBN: 0 7458 0689 9

PA Consulting Group, *How to take part in the quality revolution: a management guide,* PA Consulting Group. (Undated)

Taylor et al, *CONCH: a spiral life-cycle model for KBS development, Report G, Esprit Project 1098,* Touche Ross (1989)

Wilson, Systems: *Concepts, Methodologies and Applications,* Wiley (1990),
ISBN: 0 471 92716 3

Allied Quality Assurance Publication

AQAP, AQAP - 13: *Nato Software Quality Control System Requirements.* (1981)

International Organization for Standardization

ISO, *ISO 9001 - Quality Systems: Specification for design/development, production, installation and servicing (also known as British Standard BS5750, Part 1,* British Standards Institution, (1987).

Glossary

activity	The process of creation, or further development, of a product. Each time a product is to be created or enhanced, an activity is defined to effect the transformation.
activity description	Documentation of an activity. It is a description of the activity which includes its purpose and the required inputs, outputs and skills required to undertake the activity.
agent	A person or other system that interacts with or is a component of the KBS.
Application Requirements Model	The product that holds a specification of the required external behaviour of the system, together with the organisational, operational, technical and resource constraints which affect the way that the system is to be designed and implemented.
BAC	See Business Assurance Co-ordinator.
Business Assurance Co-ordinator (BAC)	A role within the Project Assurance Team that is responsible for planning, monitoring and reporting on all administrative aspects of the project. The role acts as the focal point for administrative controls.
Business Domain Model	The product that provides an understanding of the organisational structure and business functions. This understanding allows the scope of possible applications to be identified. The impact of a possible system on the organisation can be clarified and defined. For potential applications the Business Domain Model covers both current and proposed systems and requirements.
CCTA Risk Analysis and Management Method (CRAMM)	A method which provides a structured and consistent basis to identify and justify all the protective measures necessary to ensure the security of both current and future IT systems used for processing data.

Checkpoint Report	A report prepared by the Project Manager, with help from the PAT, to summarise project progress which is passed to the Project Controller.
Circuit Initiation Document (CID)	The product which gathers together the information needed to control the work which is to be undertaken during a circuit of the spiral model. This information includes defining the objectives and boundaries of the activities.
Configuration Librarian	The role responsible for planning, monitoring and reporting on all configuration management aspects of the project.
configuration management	A set of techniques and procedures to record, monitor and control the status of pre-defined items which must be developed through the lifetime of the project.
CRAMM	See CCTA Risk Analysis and Management Method.
deliverables	Products which must be developed by the supply side and formally accepted by the demand side. These products must be defined in terms of content, structure and format.
demand side	The business areas within an organisation which make demands upon the IS provider(s) for the provision of information systems and services.
Development Team	The team responsible for developing the products of specific development activities within a project.
Domain Team	The team responsible for providing information for use in analysis and design activities. The team is made up of the User and Expert roles.
estimating	Calculating the approximate size of a task in terms of required resources, cost and timescale.
Executive	A role within the Project Board (usually the chairman) responsible for ensuring that the project objectives are met and that the project is completed within the approved cost and timescales.

Exception Plan	The product which documents the details of an exception situation which has arisen, or is likely to arise, including extremes that have been examined or considered, and proposes corrective action.
expert	A person who has detailed understanding in the domain of knowledge for which the KBS is to be designed. The role, *Expert,* is undertaken by a group of experts, or their representative, who provide information, during analysis and design, by interviews or by documentary evidence such as manuals or case studies.
Expertise Model	The product which holds a structured description of the knowledge (expertise) to be encoded into the implemented KBS.
Feasibility Report	The final report resulting from a feasibility study. The Feasibility Report forms the basis of management decisions about the future of the system under study.
Feasibility Study (FS)	This activity generates an initial assessment of the feasibility of building a system in the area of business which has been identified by a strategy study or project review activities.
Functional Design Model	The product which reflects design decisions concerning how individual components of the system will be implemented. It is a revision of the Logical Analysis Model.
Human-Computer Interaction (HCI)	All aspects of the interaction between computers and their users.
knowledge acquisition	A term commonly applied to the process by which KBS project teams gain an understanding of the knowledge in the business area of concern.
knowledge based systems (KBS)	Computer systems which are characterised by their ability to hold and make available knowledge in a specific domain.
Knowledge Engineer	The role of development personnel in a KBS project. They carry out the analysis, design and programming activities for a KBS development.

knowledge representation	The formalisms that are adopted to record expertise in a structured form.
Logical Analysis (LA)	This activity specifies precisely what is needed to meet the requirements without being constrained by how the requirements are to be met.
Logical Analysis Model	The pivotal product in a GEMINI-based project. It brings together the Expertise Model and the Modality Model into a single validated whole.
Logical Design (LD)	This activity completes and checks all aspects of the design before implementation issues are considered in Physical Design.
Management Risk Assessment	The product used to document the risk assessment undertaken during the risk assessment sector of the spiral model.
Modality Model	The product which defines interactions in the proposed system. *Agents* are persons or processes that interact with or are components of the proposed system. The Modality Model identifies the agents, defines which tasks each performs and how they can ask for or give information. The pattern of interaction between agents is termed *modality*.
object orientation	The object-oriented paradigm is an approach to modelling which builds on ideas of abstract (real world) objects, encapsulation and class inheritance. • An *object* contains both data, represented by attributes, and processing, represented by methods. The 'object' behaves (performs a task) in response to receiving a message that it understands • A *method* is an internally coded procedure which implements (part of) the functionality of an object. It is actioned when the object receives a specific message

- *Encapsulation*, also known as 'information hiding', ensures that the internal structure of an object is invisible to all other objects. Encapsulation isolates the object data and methods from the outside world. All communication between objects is in the form of messages
- A *message* is the mechanism by which one object communicates with another to force the execution of a method
- A *class* is used to define common attributes and methods for a group of objects. The "class object" can be considered as a parent of the (child) objects it relates to. A child may have more than one parent
- *Inheritance* is the hierarchic mechanism by which "child" objects exhibit behaviour and properties defined by their forebears.

See Booch (1991), Meyer (1988) and Rumbaugh (1991).

PAT	See Project Assurance Team.
PBS	See Product Breakdown Structure.
PFD	See Product Flow Diagram.
Physical Design (PD)	This activity generates the Physical Design Model in sufficient detail to enable development of the operational system.
Physical Design Model	The product which represents all the components and functions of the system to be implemented. It is implementation dependent, the design details being dependent on the technical environment chosen for implementation.
Physical Environment Specification	The product which specifies the hardware and software products and services to be supplied, commissioned and made available for implementation.
Physical System Specification	The product that draws together the Physical Design Model and the Physical Environment Specification.

PID	See Project Initiation Document.
PIR	See Post Implementation Review
plan	The product that documents the results of the planning process. It shows targets in terms of products, resources required, timescales and quality. It shows how the resources identified have been scheduled to meet these targets.
planning	The process of estimating, collating, sequencing and scheduling the project's resources to deliver the required products.
Post Implementation Review (PIR)	A formal mechanism to determine the extent to which a completed project has met its objectives and realised the expected benefits. It generally takes place about 6 months after implementation.
PRINCE	A government developed method for project management with particular application to the management of Information Systems projects. It is a development of the PROMPT method which has been in use in government departments since 1983.
product	Any output from a project. The output may be an item of software, hardware, or documentation and may itself consist of a number of detailed products. In GEMINI, products are described within three main categories: *Management Products* (which are produced during the management of a project), *Technical Products* (which are those products that make up the system) and *Quality Products* (which are produced for, or by, the quality process).
Product Breakdown Structure (PBS)	The product which identifies the products which are required and must be produced by a project. It describes the system in a hierarchic way, decomposing it through a number of levels down to the components of each product.
product description	The product which describes the purpose, form and components of a product, and lists the quality criteria which apply to it.

Product Flow Diagram (PFD)	The product which is used to describe the technical strategy of a project in terms of a diagram showing the products of the project and how they are derived from each other. It is essentially a working document produced by planners for their own benefit.
production management	The activities to administer all the resources needed to develop the Technical Products which are required to fulfil the objectives of the project.
product quality review	A means whereby a product (or group of related products) is checked against an agreed set of quality criteria. Those criteria are defined for every product (on the product description) and may be supplemented with other documents.
Progress Report	The product which is used to report back to management details of the current status of the project, highlighting relevant issues.
Project Assurance Team (PAT)	The team that assists the Project Controller by ensuring that the project products are fit for their intended purpose and conform to specification. The PAT must ensure that quality management is undertaken within the project. The Project Assurance Team comprises: • Business Assurance Co-ordinator (BAC) • Technical Assurance Co-ordinator (TAC) • User Assurance Co-ordinator (UAC).
Project Board	A group of senior managers within the demand side organisation who have an interest in, and overall control of, the KBS project. The Project Board must provide overall guidance and direction to the project. The Project Board comprises: • Executive • Senior User • Senior Technical.

Project Controller	The demand side project manager responsible for the success of the project in terms of the quality of the delivered system, budget and timescale. The Project Controller acts on behalf of the Project Board, has close links with the board members and attends board meetings.
Project Evaluation Report	The product which provides an indication of how successful the project has been in all its various aspects.
project integration	The development of an implementable system which combines KBS and conventional IT. Integration may involve techniques for the analysis and design, or techniques and tools for implementation.
Project Initiation Document (PID)	The product approved by the Project Board at project initiation; it defines the terms of reference and objectives for the project. It is used to identify business requirements, as well as organisational and general information needs, security aspects and an initial Project Plan.
project management	The activities to administer all resources to develop products which are required to fulfil the objectives of the project.
project management process model	An iterative approach to project management for KBS development projects. This model incorporates four sectors concerning the activities of risk assessment, planning, development and review.
Project Manager	A role with day-to-day responsibility for ensuring that the supply side produces the required products, to the required standard of quality, within specified constraints of time and cost.
project organisation	The composition of a project team in terms of the skills and experience required to undertake all of the necessary functions of control, management and development within a project.
QA	See quality assurance.
QAS	See quality assurance statement.

quality	Quality is defined in ISO 8402 as: *the totality of features and characteristics of a product or service that bear on its ability to satisfy stated or implied needs.*
quality assurance (QA)	The scope of quality assurance is described in ISO 8402 - 1986. It covers: *all those planned and systematic actions that provide adequate confidence that a product or service will satisfy given requirements for quality.*
quality assurance statement (QAS)	This product documents the quality approach for the project. It is developed by the Project Controller to specify quality issues which must be addressed throughout the project.
quality control	The mechanisms to encompass the operational techniques and activities for use in satisfying the project and product requirements.
quality criteria	The identifiable characteristics of a product that are to be examined to determine whether the product meets stated requirements and can be considered fit for its purpose. These characteristics are documented in a product description for each product.
quality management	The practice of a variety of tasks which for individual projects, assure and control development activities through the use of various techniques, including reviews, walkthroughs and inspections.
quality review	An examination to confirm that products conform to their specification. Errors found in products are documented and corrected.
Requirements Analysis (RA)	This activity specifies requirements early in the project to establish a sound basis for design and acceptance.

Review Team	A group of people who undertake the quality review of a product. There will be a chairman for the Review Team as well as a presenter (originator of the material to be reviewed). The remainder of the team includes people who must assess the product from a particular perspective to ensure that it is fit for purpose.
risk	In a project *risk* is the likelihood, and impact, of a project *failing* to: • meet a business need and provide expected business benefits • prove technically feasible • prove organisationally feasible • complete on time and within budget • develop products which meet requirements.
risk assessment	The process of identifying risks, evaluating their impact and identifying countermeasures.
risk management	The process by which risks, inherent in a project and its environment, are identified, understood, analysed and addressed.
role	One of the discrete project functions required to manage and carry out a project. Roles are assigned to individuals according to the needs of the project and the mix of skills available.
Selected Application Model	The product which provides a representation of the tasks and data flows in an application. This representation provides a more precise definition of the functionality of the proposed application than the Business Domain Model.
Senior Technical	The role on the Project Board that represents the interests of demand side areas which have responsibility for technical implementation of the KBS, and for computer services support during its operational life.

Senior User	The role on the Project Board that represents the interests of all user departments and functions affected by the project. In addition, the Senior User monitors project progress against the business requirements of user management.
spiral model	See project management process model.
supply side	Those responsible for providing information systems to meet the needs of the demand side business.
system maintenance	All activities concerned with making any change, however small, to an existing computer system.
System Modelling (SM)	This activity defines the business environment around the proposed application in detail so that the application impact on the business can be established accurately.
TAC	See Technical Assurance Co-ordinator
Team Leader	The role responsible for managing a Development Team and specific resources during the development of particular products.
Technical Assurance Co-ordinator (TAC)	The role within the Project Assurance Team responsible for planning, monitoring and reporting on all technical assurance aspects of the project. The role ensures that the technical and operating standards defined for the project and its products are used to good effect.
Technical Environment Definition (TE)	This activity generates a detailed assessment of the technical environment for implementation of the application.
Technical Environment Description (TED)	This product contains a definition of the requirements of the environment in which the application is to be developed and will run.
Technical Environment Options	This product describes the reasonable options for the implementation of the system, in sufficient detail to support choice.
TED	See Technical Environment Description.

UAC	See User Assurance Co-ordinator.
user	Any person who uses a system for business purposes. The role, *User*, is undertaken by a group of users, or their representative, who provides information, during analysis and design, on user requirements and may be involved in testing.
User Assurance Co-ordinator (UAC)	The role within the Project Assurance Team responsible for monitoring and reporting on the user assurance aspects of the project. In addition, the role represents the user on a day-to-day basis.
work structure	A diagram that shows the activities, and flows of products, which must be undertaken to develop the required project products.

Index

Printed in the United Kingdom for HMSO
Dd 297512 11/93 C7 531/3 12521